SAKANA & TSUKIJI BOOK

野村　祐三　著

魚＆築地市場　ガイドブック
《英語対訳つき》

INTRODUCTION

はじめに

「日本の魚は特別においしい」と内外ともに広く知られています。なぜ特別なのか？ 理由の一つは日本列島が海流に恵まれていることにあります。南からは暖流の「黒潮」が流れて多種多様な魚を運んできます。北からは親潮とリマン海流が北の魚と栄養たっぷりの餌を持ってきます。だから南と北の身質のよい魚が育つのです。加えて漁獲後のていねいな魚の扱いや水揚げから消費者に届くまでの鮮度保持の工夫が、魚のおいしさを維持します。また江戸前寿司などが「おいしい」に一役買っているのは言うまでもありません。本書ではそんな魅力あふれる日本の魚を紹介します。

It is well known that "Japanese fishes are especially delicious" both within and outside Japan. Why are they special? One of the reasons is that the Japan islands is blessed with ocean currents. From the south, the Black Hot Current carries various kinds of fish. From the north, the Oyashio Current and the Liman Cold Current bring northern fish and nutrient-rich food. Therefore, northern and southern fishes thrive here. In addition to this, the careful treatment of fish after catching and the elaboration to keep its freshness from landing to delivering to consumers help to preserve the good taste of fish. It goes without saying that Edomae-sushi plays an important role for its reputation. This book introduces such Japanese fish full of attraction.

the SAKANA&TSUKIJI BOOK

魚&築地市場 ガイドブック

CONTENTS

Chapter 1

ALL ABOUT FISHES
魚大全

Chapter 2

JAPANESE FISH MARKET
魚市場を知る

Chapter 3
FISHING PORT AND MARKET
日本の漁港・市場

Chapter 4

JAPANESE FISH DISHES
日本の魚料理

THE
TSUKIJI OUTER MARKET

築地場外市場

築地市場は、プロが買い付けを行う「場内」と一般人向けに開放されている「場外」の2つのエリアに分かれている。場内では、プロの業者向けにせりや卸売り用の生鮮食品などの販売を行っているが、場外では、一般の人も買い物や食事が楽しめる。プロの信頼も厚い高品質の商品を気軽に購入することができ、新鮮な食材を使った食事をリーズナブルに楽しむこともできる。

There are two areas in Tsukiji Market: the inner market called "Jonai" and the outer one called "Jogai". "Jonai" is the wholesale market for professionals. Venders put seafood to the auctions or sell perishables in each shop to the professionals there. On the other hand, "Jogai", the outer market, is open to ordinary customers and visitors. They can enjoy shopping and eating there. At the outer market, you can buy high-quality merchandise lightheartedly which the professionals put strong faith in. You can also enjoy tasting dishes which are made from fresh ingredients at reasonable prices.

SHOPS IN THE TSUKIJI OUTER MARKET

築地場外市場のお店

400軒もの店が軒を連ねる築地場外市場。早朝にオープンし昼過ぎには閉店する店も多いので、午前中の買い物がおすすめ。魚を知り尽くしたプロの味を食べて、買って歩こう。

There are as many as 400 stores in the Tsukiji Outer Market. It is better to go shopping in the morning because many shops are open early and close just past noon. Let's enjoy shopping and eating premium taste!

TSUKIJI SUSHI-ICHIBAN
TSUKIJI JYOGAI ICHIBA CHUO-TEN

築地　すし一番　築地場外市場中央店

築地でマグロを楽しみたいならベストな名店。極上マグロを一本買いしており豊富なメニューも魅力。一番名物は真赤に輝く新鮮なマグロの赤身がたっぷりのった「とろ鉄火丼」。

The best restaurant to taste tuna in Tsukiji. They have a wide variety on the menu, buying an extra fine tuna whole. Their special dish is "Torotekka-Don" with a lot of fresh red tuna.

Shop data

☎ 03-3524-7188　🕐 24時間　休 無休　URL http://sakanaya-group.com/04sushiichiban/00top/main.html
Tel:03-3524-7188　**Hours**:24 hours　**Closed**:Nothing　**URL**:http://sakanaya-group.com/04sushiichiban/00top/main.html

UOGASHI-DON KANNO

うおがし丼かんの

店主自らせり場で買い付けした新鮮なネタを使ったどんぶりを45種類ほど取りそろえる。500円から楽しめるリーズナブルさも魅力。自慢は、マグロ・ウニ・イクラが満載の「うおがし丼」。

They serve about 45 kinds of Donburi at reasonable prices with fresh topping bought by the owner. Their vaunted menu is "Uogashi-Don" full with tuna, sea urchin and salmon roe.

Shop data

☎ 03-3546-0300　🕐 8:00 〜 16:00　休 無休　URL なし
Tel:03-3546-0300　**Hours**:8:00-16:30　**Closed**:Nothing　**URL**:Nothing

ISESHO

伊勢正

昆布や干し貝柱、干ししいたけなど和食店で使用されている高級国産食材の、形くずれ廉価版を購入できる。かつお節、削り節、煮干しなども豊富に取り揃え、和の醍醐味を堪能できる。

They sell shape-imperfect products of luxury domestic food that is used in the Japanese-style restaurant at reasonable prices. You can see the best part of Japanese food.

Shop data

☎ 03-3541-5551　⏰ 5:00 〜 13:00　🚫 市場定休日　URL http://iseshou.com/
Tel:03-3541-5551　**Hours:**5:00-13:00　**Closed:**Days when the market closed　**URL:**http://iseshou.com/

TSUKIJI EDOICHI
HONTEN

築地　江戸一　本店

佃煮と煮豆をメインに取り扱う創業100年の老舗。江戸前佃煮の伝統の味にこだわりつづけ、江戸の食文化を継承している。一番人気は、ホタテを秘伝のタレで炊き上げた「一口ほたて」。

An old shop established a hundred years ago. They mainly sell food boiled down in soy and boiled beans, carrying on the food culture of Edo. "Hitokuchi Hotate" is the most popular.

Shop data

☎ 03-3543-5225　⏰ 8:00 〜 14:00　🚫 日・祝、市場定休日　URL http://edo1-iida.p-kit.com/
Tel:03-3543-5225　**Hours:**8:30-14:00　**Closed:**Sundays, Holidays, Days when the market closed　**URL:**http://edo1-iida.p-kit.com/

TSUKIJI
DONBURI ICHIBA

築地どんぶり市場

魚介の他にも洋風の丼を取り揃える専門店。種類豊富なメニューを低価格で提供している。柔らかくクセになる味付けが抜群のマグロほほ肉ステーキ丼を味わうことができる。

A Donburi specialty restaurant which have not only seafood bowl but also western-style bowl. You can eat various bowls at reasonable prices. Tuna cheek stake bowl is addictive.

Shop data

☎ 03-3541-8978　⏰ 月・火 4:30 〜 15:00、水〜土24時間　🚫 日・祝　URL なし
Tel:03-3541-8978　**Hours:**4:30-15:00 (Monday, Tuesday), 24 hours (from Wednesday to Satureday)　**Closed:**Sundays and Holiday　**URL:**Nothing

1590　　1596~　　1657~　　1679　　1857~　　1923

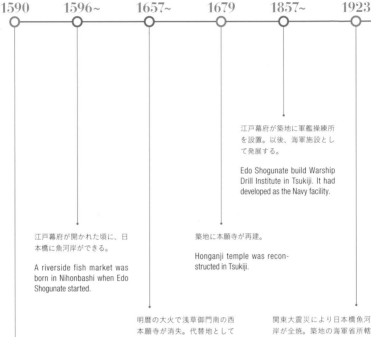

江戸幕府が築地に軍艦操練所を設置。以後、海軍施設として発展する。

Edo Shogunate build Warship Drill Institute in Tsukiji. It had developed as the Navy facility.

江戸幕府が開かれた頃に、日本橋に魚河岸ができる。

A riverside fish market was born in Nihonbashi when Edo Shogunate started.

築地に本願寺が再建。

Honganji temple was reconstructed in Tsukiji.

明暦の大火で浅草御門南の西本願寺が消失。代替地として造成された埋め立て地が「築地」と呼ばれるようになる。

Nishi-Honganji temple was burned down in the Great Fire of Meireki. The reclaimed land which was built as an alternative place became called Tsukiji.

関東大震災により日本橋魚河岸が全焼。築地の海軍省所轄地を借り受け、臨時魚市場が再開される。

The riverside fish market in Nihonbashi was burned down in the Great Kanto Earthquake. It resumed as a temporary fish market, borrowing the space under the Navy.

摂津国佃村の漁師が徳川家康の要請で江戸に移住する。

Fishermen who lived in Tsukuda village, Settu Province immigrated to Edo, requesting from Tokugawa Ieyasu.

History of

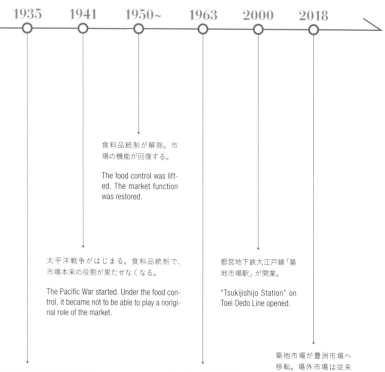

1935   1941   1950~   1963   2000   2018

食料品統制が解除。市
場の機能が回復する。

The food control was lift-
ed. The market function
was restored.

太平洋戦争がはじまる。食料品統制で、
市場本来の役割が果たせなくなる。

The Pacific War started. Under the food control, it became not to be able to play a norigi-
nal role of the market.

都営地下鉄大江戸線「築
地市場駅」が開業。

"Tsukijishijo Station" on
Toei Oedo Line opened.

築地市場が豊洲市場へ
移転。場外市場は従来
通り残る。

Tsukiji Market relocated
to Toyosu Market. The
outer market "Jogai"
goes as in the past.

東京市中央卸売市場（築地市
場）が正式に開設。

The Tokyo central wholesale
market (Tsukiji Market) was of-
ficially open.

東京メトロ日比谷線「築
地駅」が開業。

"Tsukiji Station" on the
Tokyo Metro Hibiya Line
opened.

THE TSUKIJI OUTER MARKET

TSUKIJI

THE DATA ABOUT TSUKIJI MARKET

数字で知る築地市場

(1) About 480 kinds of seafood are traded.
約480種類の水産物を取り扱う。

(2) About 42,000 visitors per day.
1日当たりの入場人員は約4万2000人。

(3) About 19,000 of admission vehicles per day.
1日当たりの入場車両数は約1万9000台。

(4) The water usage is about 8,300 cubic meters per day.
1日当たりの水使用量は約8300立方メートル。

(5) The electricity usage is about 1,316,000 kWh per day.
1日当たりの電気使用量は約13万1600kWh。

(6) The total site area of approximately 23 hectares— about 5 times the area of Tokyo Dome.
敷地面積約23ヘクタール。東京ドームの約5個分!

(7) The annual trading volume of seafood is 436,274 tons, the annual amount of it is 440,145,000,000 yen.
水産物の年間の取扱数量は43万6274トン、金額にして4401億4500万円。

(8) The parking capacity is about 4,710 cars.
駐車場施設の駐車可能台数は約4710台。

(9) The storage capacity of refrigerating facility is about 21,960 tons.
冷蔵庫施設の冷蔵収容能力は約2万1960トン。

「築地市場概要 平成28年度版(東京都中央卸売市場築地市場)」より

ALL ABOUT FISHES

魚大全

CLASSIFICATION OF FISH

魚 の 分 類

TUNA
⇒ P.020-025

マグロ

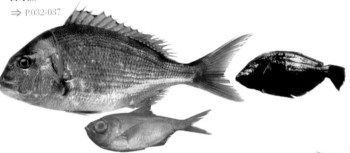

WHITE FISH

白身魚
⇒ P.032-037

CRAB·SHRIMP

カニ・エビ
⇒ P.040-045

日本では体表が青いアジやイワ
シなどを「青魚」、赤身肉のマ
グロやカツオを「赤身魚」、身
肉が白いヒラメやカレイなどを
「白身」に分類する。

In Japan, fishes with the blue surface of the body are classified in
"bluefishes", ones with red flesh
are classified in "red meat fishes",
and ones are classified in "white-
fishes".

SQUID·OCTPUS
イカ・タコ　⇒ P.046-051

RIVER FISH
川魚
⇒ P.038-039

SHELL AND OTHERS
貝・その他
⇒ P.052-058

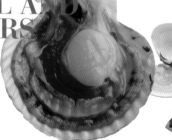

BLUE FISH
青魚
⇒ P.026-031

PACIFIC BLUEFIN TUNA

クロマグロ

⚠ 大きな体にしては
眼が小さい。
Eyes are small in contrast
to its big body.

単に「マグロ」といえば多くはクロマグロを指す。市場関係者や寿司屋では「ホンマグロ」と呼ぶ。日本人がもっとも好む魚だ。日本近海のクロマグロは台湾沖で生まれ、黒潮と対馬海流に乗りながら成長する。北に行くほど脂がのり、北海道や青森県産が最高級品として取引される。世界中の産地から大消費国の日本に運ばれてくる。

"Maguro", a favorite sushi topping in Japan, usually means pacific bluefin tuna. Market participants and sushi chefs call it "Hon Maguro". Tuna which is caught in the sea near Japan is born off the coast of Taiwan and grow up moving with the Black Current and Tsushima Current. Tunas from Hokkaido or Aomori Prefecture are rated the highest because of its fattiness.

KUROMAGURO

黒鮪

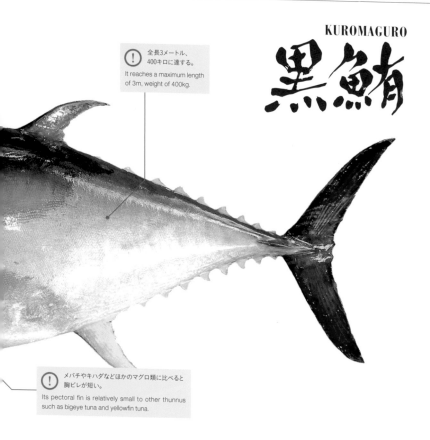

(!) 全長3メートル、
400キロに達する。

It reaches a maximum length
of 3m, weight of 400kg.

(!) メバチやキハダなどほかのマグロ類に比べると
胸ビレが短い。

Its pectoral fin is relatively small to other thunnus
such as bigeye tuna and yellowfin tuna.

The king of fish!
Delicious tuna from the sea
near Japan is most popular

魚の王者！ 日本近海産は美味この上なく
寿司だねの一番人気

分類	スズキ目サバ科マグロ属	旬	10～2月	料理	刺身、寿司、ねぎま鍋、和えぬた、山かけ	Class:	Perciformes, Scombridae, Thunnus

Season: October-February Dish: Sashimi, Sushi, Hot pot with scallion, With vinegared miso , With grated Japanese yam

THE PARTS OF PACIFIC BLUEFIN TUNA

クロマグロの部位

背 dorsum
ハナレミ hanaremi
中トロ medium fatty tuna
赤身 red meat
血合い fish meat with a bloody color
トロ fatty tuna
大トロ fattiest portion of tuna
腹 venter

背の一番 first part of middle back
背の二番 second part of middle back
背カミ upper back
背シモ bottom back
腹シモ bottom abdomen
カマ collar of a fish
腹カミ upper abdomen
腹ナカ first part of middle abdomen
腹コシ second part of middle abdomen

クロマグロは部位によって食味と価格が大きく分かれる。大別すると大トロと中トロ、赤身の三つの部位になる。人気の大トロは腹部にあり、脂がたっぷりとのって珍重される。特に「腹カミ」といわれる部分の大トロは最高級品として、多くが高級料亭や高級寿司店に買われていく。脂が適度にのる中トロ、味わい深い赤身を好むマグロ好きも少なくない。

The taste and price of Pacific bluefin tuna vary with its portion. It can be divided into three parts: otoro, chutoro and akami. Otoro which is the fattiest portion of tuna is most popular and especially harakami, extra fatty part of otoro, is the finest portion which Japanese high class restaurants eager to buy. Quite a few people like medium fattiness of chutoro or deep flavor of akami (red meat).

TUNA FISHERY MAP

マグロの漁場マップ

- ❶ 沖縄　Okinawa
- ❷ 五島列島　Goto Islands
- ❸ 壱岐　Iki
- ❹ 対馬　Tsushima
- ❺ 萩・見島　Hagi,Mishima
- ❻ 室戸沖　Muroto oki
- ❼ 日ノ御崎　Hinomisaki
- ❽ 明石海峡　Akashi Strait
- ❾ 黒潮周辺　Kuroshio around
- ❿ 銚子沖　Choshi oki

秋から冬／
Autumn to Winter

夏から冬／
From summer to winter

Tsushima current
対馬海流

夏／Summer

春／Spring

Kuroshio current
黒潮

春／Spring

産卵場所

- ⓫ 佐渡島　Sado Island
- ⓬ 飛島　Tobi Island
- ⓭ 久六島　Kyuroku Island
- ⓮ 松前　Matsumae
- ⓯ 竜飛崎　Tappizaki
- ⓰ 大間崎　Omazaki
- ⓱ 天売島　Teuri Island
- ⓲ 金華山沖　Kinkazan oki
- ⓳ 三陸沖　Sanriku oki
- ⓴ 泊沖　Tomari oki

BIGEYE TUNA
メバチ

「メバチマグロ」とも呼ばれる。クロマグロとミナミマグロに次いで市場価値が高い。スーパーに柵や刺身のパックで並ぶのは、このメバチとキハダが多い。クロマグロにくらべると身の赤色がうすく食感がやわらかい。

Bigeye tuna, also called "Mebachi Maguro", has a high market value after pacific bluefin tuna and southern bluefin tuna. In comparison with pacific bluefin tuna, it has a lighter red color and its texture is softer.

分類 スズキ目サバ科マグロ属 旬 6〜8月 料理 刺身、寿司、和えぬた、山かけ、鉄火丼 **Class:**Perciformes, Scombridae, Thunnus.
Season: June-August **Dish:**Sashimi, Sushi, With vinegared miso, With grated Japanese yam, A bowl of vinegared rice with slices of raw tuna

SOUTHERN BLUEFIN TUNA
ミナミマグロ

インド洋やオーストラリア海域で多く漁獲され「インドマグロ」とも呼ばれる。旨味が強くて肉質がよく締まる。寿司だねとしてクロマグロ同様に評価される。日本にはオーストラリア産の蓄養ものが多く輸入されている。

It is called "Indo Maguro" and almost caught in the Indian Ocean or the sea around Australia. It has a strong flavor and relatively firmer flesh, rated high as sushi topping like pacific bluefin tuna.

分類 スズキ目サバ科マグロ属 旬 4〜9月（蓄養） 料理 刺身、寿司、山かけ、鉄火丼 **Class:**Perciformes, Scombridae, Thunnus
Season: April-September (culture fish) **Dish:**Sashimi, Sushi, With grated Japanese yam, A bowl of vinegared rice with slices of raw tuna

YELLOWFIN TUNA
キハダ

KIHADA

黄肌

キハダは「キハダマグロ」とも「キワダ」とも呼ばれる。体が黄色みを帯び、特に第二背ビレと尻ビレが黄色い。身は赤みがうすく桃色に近い。クロマグロに比べるとうま味に欠けるが、関西ではその淡泊さで好まれる。

This is called both "Kihada Mauro" and "Kiwada". The lean cut has a pink color. The umami flavor of it is slighter than pacific bluefin tuna but its plainer flavors entertain people especially in the Kansai region.

分類 スズキ目サバ科マグロ属 **旬** 7 ～ 8月 **料理** 刺身、寿司、和えぬた、山かけ、鉄火丼 **Class:** Perciformes, Scombridae, Thunnus **Season:** July-August **Dish:** Sashimi, Sushi, With vinegared miso, With grated Japanese yam, A bowl of vinegared rice with slices of raw tuna

ALBACORE
ビンナガ

BINNAGA

鬢長

大きくても体長1・4メートル、体重40キロとマグロの仲間としては小型。「ビンチョウ」とも呼ばれる。身は淡い桃色。回転寿司によく利用され「ビントロ」と呼ばれる腹部は手頃な価格と脂ののりのよさで注文が多い。

This fish is comparatively small species in Thunnus. It is also called "Bincho" and its flesh is pale pink. The abdomen called "Bintoro" is popular because of the affordable price and fattiness.

分類 スズキ目サバ科マグロ属 **旬** 4 ～ 6月 **料理** 刺身、寿司、照り焼き **Class:** Perciformes, Scombridae, Thunnus **Season:** April-June **Dish:** Sashimi, Sushi, Broiled with soy sauce (Teriyaki)

HORSE MACKEREL

アジ

全長40センチに達するが、寿司には15～20センチが向いている。

It reached 40 meters in height. Smallish ones around 15 to 20 centimeters is good to use for sushi.

単に「アジ」といえばマアジを指す。日本近海のマアジには二つのグループがある。一つはまき網漁で大量に漁獲される回遊性のマアジ。ほっそりとして全体に黒っぽく「黒あじ」とも呼ばれる。もう一つは浅瀬に生息する瀬付きアジ。ずんぐりして背や尾のあたりが黄色みを帯び「黄あじ」の別名がある。脂がよくのり美味だが、水揚げ量が少なく高価。

When it is simply called "Aji", it usually means horse mackerel. It can be divided into two groups. One is "Kuroaji" with slender and blackish body, migratory wondering fish caught in a large quantities by round haul net. The other is "Kiaji", one of shallow water, which has a blocky body with yellowish back and caudal fin. It is delicious with plenty of fat but expensive because of small catch.

AJI

鯵

> (!) 側線に沿って
> 「ゼンゴ」と呼ばれるかたいウロコが走る。
> There are hard scales called "Zengo" along a lateral line.

Cheap fish for the masses but distinctive bluefish flavor is formidable

手頃価格の大衆魚だが
青魚特有の味わいはあなどれない

分類 スズキ目アジ科マアジ属　旬 5 ～ 9月　料理 刺身、たたき、寿司、南蛮漬け、塩焼き、煮魚、フライ　**Class:**Perciformes, Carangidae, Horse mackerel **Season:**May-September **Dish:**Sashimi, Finely chopped, Sushi, Nanbanzuke, Grilled with salt, Boiled, Fried

SARDINE
イワシ

日本でよく食べられるイワシはマイワシ、ウルメイワシ、カタクチイワシの3種類。単に「イワシ」といえば体側に黒い星模様が並ぶマイワシを指す。代表的な大衆魚だが、生でよく、煮ても焼いても揚げてもうまい。

Japanese people often eat three kinds of sardine; Japanese sardine, Round herring, Anchovy. "Iwashi" usually means Japanese sardine with a black star pattern on its side. It is good to eat raw, boiled and grilled.

分類 ニシン目ニシン科マイワシ属　旬 4～6月　料理 刺身、塩焼き、丸干し、フライ、卯の花ずし、ごま漬け　**Class:** Clupeiformes, Clupeidae, Sardinops　**Season:** April-June　**Dish:** Sashimi, Grilled with salt, Whole dried fish, Fried, A flower of deutzia-sushi, Vinegared with sesame

SKIPJACK TUNA
カツオ

カツオは回遊魚だ。3月下旬に四国南方に現れ、紀伊半島、伊豆・房総、常磐・三陸沖へと走る。この群れは「上りがつお」と呼ばれる。10月頃に三陸沖で南下するグループは「下りがつお」。それぞれのうまさを持つ。

It is called "Nobori gatsuo", when migrating northward from the coast of Shikoku to Sanriku late in March, When moving southward about October, it is called "Kudari gatsuo". Each of them has a distinctive taste.

分類 スズキ目サバ科カツオ属　旬 4～5月、9～10月　料理 土佐造り(たたき)、なまり節、びんた料理　**Class:** Perciformes, Scombridae, Katsuwonus　**Season:** April-May, September-October　**Dish:** Seared and eat with soy source, Boiled and half-dried, Cooked jowl

GIZZARD SHAD
コノシロ

体長4〜5センチはシンコ、中型はコハダ、15センチ以上はコノシロと成長段階ごとに呼び分けられる。寿司だねにはシンコやコハダが向く。ハシリのシンコは希少で、驚くほど高価に取り引きされ、よく話題になる。

Smaller one is called Shinko, one of a middle size is Kohada and bigger one is Konoshiro. The former two size are goof for sushi. The first Shinko of the season is valuable and its deal with surprising high price often gets into the news.

分類 ニシン目ニシン科コノシロ属 **旬** 10〜2月 (コハダ)、6〜7月 (シンコ) **料理** 酢のもの、寿司、粟漬け **Class:** Clupeiformes, Clupeidae, Konosirus **Season:** October-February (Kohada), June-July (Shinko) **Dish:** Vinegared, Sushi, Marinated with vinegar and millet

MACKEREL
サバ

単に「サバ」と言えばマサバを指す。「ホンサバ」とも呼ばれる。北海道から沖縄まで広く分布し、日本でもっとも親しまれている魚といえる。よく似た種類にゴマサバがある。こちらは側線下に小豆大の斑紋を持つ。

When it is simply called "Saba", it usually means chub mackerel. It is also referred to as "Honsaba". Widely distributed from Hokkaido to Okinawa, it is one of the famous fish in Japan.

分類 スズキ目サバ科サバ属 **旬** 10〜1月 **料理** しめさば、さば寿司、塩焼き、味噌煮、から揚げ **Class:** Perciformes, Scombridae, Scomber **Season:** October-January **Dish:** Salted and vinegar, Rod-shaped sushi, Grilled with salt, Boiled with miso, Fritter

サンマは季節とともに日本の太平洋岸を回遊する。サンマ漁船はそれを追い、8月の北海道東沖で漁を始めて9月には三陸沖から常磐・銚子沖へ。11月になると伊豆半島沖から紀州・四国・九州の沖へ移る。北海道東沖や三陸沖のサンマが美味なのは、寒流の豊かな餌を食べて脂がよくのっているからだ。ただし伊豆半島や紀州の名産さんますしは、この沖の脂の抜けたサンマが向いている。

This fish migrates around the Pacific coast of Japan, according to seasons. With the movements of it, fishermans changes fishing place — starting in August from off the east coast of Hokkaido, in September moving from Sanriku to Joban and Choshi, in November from Izu Peninsula to Kishu, Shikoku, finally to Kyushu. One caught in Hokkaido and Sanriku is delicious because it eats a lot in a cold sea and becomes fatty.

PACIFIC SAURY
サンマ

SANMA

秋刀魚

分類 ダツ目サンマ科サンマ属　**旬** 8～10月　**料理** 塩焼き、煮魚、から揚げ、蒲焼き、さんま寿司　**Class:** Scomberesocoidea, Scomberesocidae, Cololabis　**Season:** August-October　**Dish:** Grilled with salt, Boiled, Fritter, Spitchcocked, Pressed sushi

プリは成長段階ごとに呼び名が変わる。関東では20セ
ンチ前後がワカシ、30センチ前後がイナダ、50センチ
以上がワラサ、1メートル近くがプリと呼び分けられ
る。プリは三年魚から大回遊をはじめる。春から夏に
かけて餌を求め北海道南部海域や津軽海峡へ北上。秋
には暖かい海を目指して日本沿岸海域を南下する。氷
見（ひみ・富山県）のプリが味のよさで知られる。

This fish has various name in different stage of life. In the
Kanto region, one about 20 cm in length is called
"Wakashi", one about 30 cm is "Inada", one over 50 cm
is "Warasa", and one over 100 cm is "Buri". Yellowtail
starts migrating at 3 years old. From spring to summer, it
moves northward to the north Hokkaido and Tsugaru
Channel. In autumn it goes southward in the coast of Japan seeking a hot sea. One caught at Himi (Toyama prefecture) is well known for good taste.

YELLOWTAIL

BURI

ブリ

分類 スズキ目アジ科ブリ属　**旬** 11～2月（ブリ）　**料理** 照り焼き、あら煮、ぶり大根、かぶらずし　**Class:** Perciformes, Carangidae, Seriola
Season: November-February (Buri)　**Dish:** Grilled with soy sauce and sugar, Boiled bones, Broiled with radish, Turnip fermented sushi

RED SEA BREAM

マダイ

養殖マダイには
背を中心に黒みがかるのが
見られる。

A hatchery fish is blackish around
the back.

タイ科の魚は10種類余りあるが、単に「タイ」と言えばマダイを指す。鮮やかな朱色で見ばえがよく、日本では古くから祝い魚として用いられてきた。定置網漁やはえ縄漁で多く漁獲されるが、「加太（かだ）のたい」や「鳴門だい」などの釣りものが身質のよさで珍重される。養殖ものが多く出回る。

Thought there are more than 10 types of sparidae, "Tai" usually means red sea bream. It have been used for celebratory from long ago due to its brilliant look of bright red. Some of it especially caught by pole-and-line fishing, such as "Kadanotai" and "Narutodai", is valued for its better flesh substance. Hatchery fishes is abundant on the market.

MADAI
真鯛

(!) ウロコが硬いので料理の際には徹底的に取り除くこと。

When you cook it, you must remove its hard scales.

(!) 尾ビレの後縁が黒い。近似種のキダイやチダイは黒くない。

The back edge of a caudal fin is black. Similar species such as yellowback sea bream and crimson sea bream.

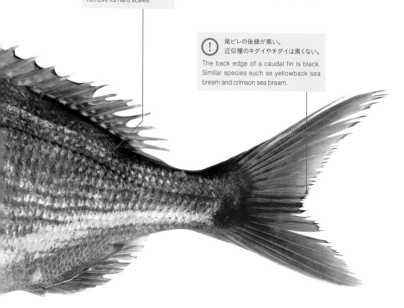

Elegant look and rich taste enhance a mood of celebratory

華やかな姿と上品な食味が祝いの気分を
ぐっと高める

分類 スズキ目タイ科マダイ属　**旬** 12〜4月　**料理** 刺身、寿司、塩焼き、かぶと煮、潮汁、たい飯　**Class:** Perciformes, Sparidae, Pagrus
Season: December-April　**Dish:** Sashimi, Sushi, Grilled with salt, Simmered head of sea beam, Thin soup, Tai-meshi

SPLENDID ALFONSINO
キンメダイ

金目魚

単に「キンメ」とも呼ばれる。全体があざやかな朱色で見ばえがよく、マダイの代わりに尾頭付きで祝い膳を飾ることがある。脂肪分が多く、煮魚にするといい味に仕上がる。西京漬けや開き干しなどの加工品がよく出回る。

Because it has an attractive look of vivid vermillion color, a whole cooked one is sometimes prepared for celebratory table as a substitute for red sea bream. The fatty flesh ends up with a great taste by boiling.

分類 キンメダイ目キンメダイ科キンメダイ属　**旬** 11〜2月　**料理** 煮魚、焼き魚、鍋、湯引き、西京漬け　**Class:** Beryciformes, Berycidae, Beryx　**Season:** November-February　**Dish:** Boiled, Grilled, A japanese stew, Parboiled, Pickled in sweet kyoto-style miso

034

JAPANESE SEA BASS
スズキ

鱸

広く日本の沿岸に生息する。成長段階ごとに名が変わり、関東では1歳魚の30センチ前後がセイゴ、2〜3歳魚の50〜60センチがフッコ、それ以上がスズキと呼び分けられる。食べ方は大きさによって違ってくる。

In the Kanto region, it has various name; the first name is "Seigo" for a fish about 30 cm in length, the second is "Fukko" for one the length of which is 50-60 cm, and the last is "Suzuki" after that.

分類 スズキ目スズキ科スズキ属　**旬** 6〜8月　**料理** から揚げ（セイゴ）、あらい（フッコ）、刺身、塩焼き（スズキ）　**Class:** Perciformes, Lateolabracidae, Lateolabrax　**Season:** June-August　**Dish:** Fritter (Seigo), Slices washed in cold water (Fukko), Sashimi, Grilled with salt (Suzuki)

FLOUNDER
ヒラメ

鮃

姿がよく似るカレイと見分ける方法に「右カレイに左ヒ
ラメ」という教えがある。眼が右側にあればカレイ、眼
が左側にあればヒラメだ。産卵前の冬に漁獲される「寒
平目」は、そのおいしさで食通をうならせる。

flatfishes and flounders look alike; the former has eyes on
the left side of the head and the latter has ones on the right
side. "Kanbirame" which is caught before spawning in winter is really delicious.

分類 カレイ目ヒラメ科ヒラメ属 旬 10〜2月 料理 刺身、寿司、ムニエル、から揚げ Class:Pleuronectiformes, Paralichthyidae,
Paralichthys Season:October-February Dish:Sashimi, Sushi, Meuniere, Fritter

MARBLED SOLE
マコガレイ

真子鰈

数あるカレイ類のなかでも味のよさで評価が高い。古く
から「その味くらべるものなし」と伝わる「城下（しろし
た）かれい」はマコガレイ。日出城跡（大分県日出町）す
ぐ下の海域に生息するため、このブランド名で呼ばれる。

Marbled sole has been well-known as "Shiroshita karei",
which means castle town flatfish, for its incomparably excellent taste. Origin of that brand-name is the place where
it lives, the coast of Hiji-jo Castle Ruins (Oita prefecture) .

分類 カレイ目カレイ科ツノガレイ属 旬 6〜9月 料理 刺身、寿司、煮魚、塩焼き、から揚げ Class:Pleuronectiformes, Pleuronectidae,
Pseudopleuronectes Season:June-September Dish:Sashimi, Sushi, Boiled, Grilled with salt, Fritter

MONKFISH
アンコウ

鮟鱇

見た目は悪い。大きな顔はひしゃげたように扁平。全身がぬめりに覆われている。ただし味のよさは折り紙付き。鍋には「アンコウの七つ道具」と呼ばれる皮、肝臓、卵巣、胃袋、ひれ、白身、あご肉のすべてが利用される。

It doesn't have a very nice appearance but it's tasty. It's body is covered with sliminess. In pot dish, it is fully used with no waste, including its skin, a liver, a ovary, a stomach, a fin, a white meat, a flesh of the jaw.

分類 アンコウ目アンコウ科アンコウ属 **旬** 11〜2月 **料理** 鍋、から揚げ、煮魚、とも和え **Class:**Lophiiformes, Lophiidae **Season:**November-February **Dish:**Pot dish, Fritter, Boiled, Dressed with its liver

ROCKFISH
カサゴ

笠子

頭が大きくて口が大きい。食べる部分は少ないが、上品な味わいを持つ。魚料理にうるさい浜の人は鯛飯を炊くときにわざわざカサゴでだしをとる。フランス・マルセイユの漁師はカサゴ入りブイヤベーズがお気に入りだ。

Rockfish has big head and mouth. An edible portion of it is small but has an elegant taste. Fishermen prepare soup with it for Tai-meshi. The bouillabaisse of it is fishermens' favorite in Marseille, France.

分類 カサゴ目フサカサゴ科カサゴ属 **旬** 11〜2月 **料理** 煮魚、塩焼き、吸いもの、から揚げ **Class:**Scorpaeniformes, Scorpaenidae, Sebastiscus **Season:**Nobember-February **Dish:**Boiled, Grilled with salt, Soup, Fritter

PIKE CONGER
ハモ

無数の骨があり、料理には骨切りが不可欠になる。三枚
におろした身の皮を残し、すばやく包丁を入れて骨を細
かく断ち切る。このワザが難しく料理人のウデの見せど
ころになる。京都と大阪で特に好まれる魚だ。

Pike conger is bony fish. When slivering it, chef cut it into
three pieces and scores quickly its meat and bone with the
skin left. This process is where chefs show their skills. It's
famous in Kyoto and Osaka. It is difficult.

分類 ウナギ目ハモ科ハモ属 **旬** 6〜7月 **料理** 照り焼き、はもちり、酢の物、吸いもの **Class:**Anguilliformes, Muraenesocidae,
Muraenesox **Season:**June-July **Dish:**Grilled with soy sauce and sugar, Parboiled, Vinegared, Soup

---

TIGER PUFFER
トラフグ

トラフグはテトロドトキシンという猛毒を持っている。
それでも多くの日本人が好んで食するのは、この奇妙な
魚でしか味わえない特別なおいしさを持っているからだ。
料理するにはフグ調理免許が必須になる。

Even though tiger puffer hoards the lethal poison tetrodo-
toxin, many Japanese eat willingly this strange fish for its
particular tastiness. It is necessary to have a license to
cook it.

分類 フグ目フグ科トラフグ属 **旬** 11〜1月 **料理** 刺身、鍋、から揚げ、ひれ酒 **Class:**Tetraodontiformes, Tetraodontidae, Takifugu
Season: November-January **Dish:**Sashimi, A pot dish, Fritter, Hot sake flavored with fish fins

単に「サケ」といえば、われわれが多く食べている標準和名シロザケを指す。ほとんどが放流ものと思っていい。人工ふ化されて3～4センチに育つと放流される。椎魚は成長しながら北東太平洋からアリューシャン列島沖、ベーリング海、カムチャッカ半島東方、北太平洋へと大回遊。さらに千島列島に沿って南下して4歳の秋に産卵のため故郷日本の川をめざしてやってくる。

When it is simply called "Sake", it usually means Shiro-zake which is often eaten in Japan. Most of it can be said to be released. The eggs of salmon are hatched under artificial conditions and the young fish around 3-4 cm in length is released into a river. It grows migrating from the northeastern Pacific, through the coast of the Aleutian Islands, the Bering Sea, the eastward of the Kamchatka Peninsula, and to the northern Pacific. And then, going south along the Kurile Islands, it comes to the home river in Japan to lay eggs in the autumn when it is 4 years old.

SALMON
サケ

SAKE

分類 サケ目サケ科サケ属　旬 9～11月　料理 ルイベ、氷頭なます、いずし　**Class:** Saimoniformes, Salmonidae, Oncorhynchus
Season: September-November　**Dish:** Cut into thin slices while frozen, Thinly-sliced and vinegared salmon head cartilage, Lactic fermentaed

SWEETFISH
アユ

AYU

鮎

天然のアユは川に生まれるとすぐ海へ
下り、数センチの稚魚になると川へも
どって成長し産卵する。希少な天然も
のは珍重され、ほとんどが料理店など
へ運ばれる。流通する多くが養殖もの
で20センチ前後が店頭に並ぶ。

Natural sweetfish goes down to a sea as
soon as its birth and returned to a river. It
is rare and valued and most of it bought
by restaurant.

分類 サケ目アユ科アユ属　**旬** 6〜8月　**料理** 塩焼き、味噌田楽、あめ煮、背ごし　**Class:**Osmeriformes, Osmeridae ,Plecoglossus
Season: June August **Dish:**Grilled with salt, Coated with miso, Boiled in sugared broth, Thiny slicing soft-boned fish for sashimi

EEL
ウナギ

UNAGI

鰻

天然ものは少なく、流通する多くは日
本各沿岸で捕獲したシラスウナギを養
殖したものだ。東京風蒲焼きでは背開
きを白焼きにし、これを蒸してからた
れをつけながら焼く。関西風では腹開
きにして、たれをつけながら焼く。

The number of natural fish is small, and
most of eel on the market are glass eels
whichare caught in the coast of Japan
and cultured.Tokyo opens the eel's back
and grills it. Kansai opens his belly and
grills a sauce.

分類 ウナギ目ウナギ科ウナギ属　**旬** 1〜12月　**料理** 蒲焼き、うな丼、うざく　**Class:**Anguilliformes, Anguillidae, Anguilla **Season:**January-
december **Dish:**Glaze-grilled, Bowl of eel and rice, Vinegared eel and cucumber

SNOW CRAB
ズワイガニ

オスの脚を左右に広げると
70〜80センチに達する。
Opening widely, legs of male
reach 70-80 cm.

産地の石川県と福井県ではズワイガニのオス
を「越前がに」、島根県と鳥取県では「松葉
がに」と呼ぶ。オスは甲羅の幅が15センチ
ほどで、メスは7〜8センチ。人気は淡泊な
身がたっぷり詰まったオスだが、産地ではメ
スもひっぱりだこだ。甲羅内側にはりつく未
成熟卵（内子）と腹に抱いた成熟卵（外子）
の食感と味が、カニ好きを夢中にさせるのだ。

Male snow crab is called "Echizengani" in
Ishikawa and Fukui and "Matsubagani" in
Shimane and Tottori. The width of its shell is
about 15 cm and that of the female is 7-8 cm.
Male is more popular for dense meat of light
taste. In the habitat, the female is also popular because the texture and taste both of im-
mature eggs and of mature attract crab fan.

ZUWAIGANI

楚蟹

近似種のベニズワイガニよりも脚にふくらみがあり、身の甘みが強い。

It has swelled legs and its meat is more sweet, in comparison to similar species, red snow crab.

Crab season opening, crab lovers go to its habitat along the sea of Japan

ズワイガニ漁解禁を迎えるとカニ好きたちは
日本海沿いの産地へ

分類 十脚目クモガニ科ズワイガニ属　**旬** 11〜2月　**料理** 刺身、塩ゆで、かにちり、甲羅焼き、味噌汁（メス）　**Class:**Decapoda, Oregoniidae, Chionoecetes　**Season:**Nobember-February　**Dish:**Sashimi,Boiled with salt, Pot dish, Grilled in the shell, Miso soup (Female)

HAIRY CRAB
ケガニ

甘みのある身と濃厚な味の「かにみそ」で人気があり、北
海道みやげの代表格。北海道の噴火湾、日高地方や釧路
周辺の沖、オホーツク海沿岸で多く漁獲される。目利き
がむずかしく、甲羅が硬く手に持って重いものを選びたい。

Hairy crab is popular for a sweet and rich taste of the innards. It's a specialty of Hokkaido. It is hard to judge which
is tastier but you had better choose heavier one with a hard
shell.

分類 十脚目クリガニ科クリガニ属 旬 3～8月 料理 塩ゆで、甲羅焼き、酢のもの	Class: Decapoda, Atelecyclidae, Erimacrus
Season: March-August Dish: Boiled with salt, Grilled in the shell, Vinegared	

042

KING CRAB
タラバガニ

殻幅25センチ、脚は1メートルに達する。豪華な外見と
あふれるほどの味わいから「カニの王様」と称賛される。
国内に流通する多くが、ロシアやアラスカからの輸入も
のだ。産地でボイルされ冷凍で日本に運ばれてくる。

The shell is about 25cm in width and the leg reaches 1 m
in length. It is called the king of crab for its splendid look
and rich taste. Most of it that can be found on the domestic
market are imported from Russia and Alaska.

分類 十脚目タラバガニ科タラバガニ属 旬 10～2月 料理 塩ゆで、焼きがに	Class: Decapoda, Lithodidae, Paralithodes Season: October-
	February Dish: Boiled with salt, Grilled

ALASKAN PINK SHRIMP
アマエビ

甘海老

標準和名はホッコクアカエビ。ねっとりした食感と濃厚な甘みを持ち、寿司だねには欠かせない。本州日本海沿岸と北海道沿岸に多く水揚げされる。鮮度が落ちやすく、水揚げされるやすみやかに運ばれたものが高値を呼ぶ。

The standard Japanese name is Hokkokuakaebi. This shrimp with sticky texture and rich sweetness is indispensable as a sushi topping. Most of it is landed on the coasts of the sea of Japan and Hokkaido.

分類 十脚目タラバエビ科タラバエビ属　旬 12〜2月　料理 刺身、寿司　Class:Decapoda, Pandalidae, Pandalus　Season:December-February　Dish:Sashimi, Sushi

JAPANESE TIGER SHRIMP
クルマエビ

車海老

江戸前寿司には欠かせない一つだ。生を握ればぷりっとした食感のあとに濃い甘みが口中にあふれる。軽くゆでてにぎれば朱色の横縞模様が美しく浮かび、上品な味わいがにじみでる。東北以南の内湾や河口近くに生息。

This is an indispensable sushi topping for Edomae-sushi. You can enjoy the rich sweetness after a nice texture of raw shrimp and an elegant taste of boiled one with a beautiful look of vermilion stripes.

分類 十脚目クルマエビ科クルマエビ属　旬 6〜10月（天然もの）　料理 刺身、てんぷら、具足煮、鬼殻焼き　Class:Decapoda, Penaeidae, Marsupenaeus　Season:June-October (Natural)　Dish:Sashimi, Tempura, Boiled with the shell, Grilled with the shell

JAPANESE SPINY LOBSTER

イセエビ

第二触角の元に発音器を持ち、手に持つと
ギーギーと威嚇する。

It has a sound organ at the base of
the second antenna and make the
rasping sounds to threaten.

日本では古くから縁起物とされ、平安時代に
は祝儀や酒宴の飾りに使われていた。今日で
もイセエビ料理は結婚式の披露宴などでテー
ブルを飾る。暖流がぶつかる岩礁の多い浅海
に生息し、底刺し網漁法で多く漁獲される。
闇夜に出漁して月夜は禁漁が決まりだ。漁師
たちは「月夜の海底は明るく、網がよく見え
てイセエビがからまないからだ」という。

It has been used as a good luck charm for a
celebratory decoration from the Heian period, especially used at wedding ceremony
nowadays. It lives in reefy shallows where a
warm current hit on. Many of them are
caught by gill nets. It's the rule to sail out fishing in the dark night and not to fishing in the
moonlight night.

ISEEBI

伊勢海老

⚠ 硬い甲には、
大小の棘が密生している。
There are a lot of large and small spines
on the hard shell.

Heating bring out the splendid vermilion look and an elegant umami taste

熱を加えると華美な朱色に変わり
上品な旨味にあふれる

分類 十脚目イセエビ科イセエビ属　旬 9〜12月　料理 姿造り、味噌汁、貝足煮、鬼殻焼き、蒸しもの　**Class:**Decapoda, Palinuridae, Panulirus **Season:**September-december **Dish:**Whole fish sashimi, Miso soup, Boiled with the shell, Grilled with the shell, Steamed

JAPANESE COMMON SQUID

スルメイカ

ⓘ ヒレ（耳）は菱形。
この形でヒレが槍型の
ヤリイカと見分けられる。

The fin of Japanese common
squid is diamond-shaped, the
one of spear squid is lance-
shaped.

日本近海のスルメイカは冬生まれと秋生ま
れ、夏生まれの３つのグループがあり、北海
道から九州までの沖を広く回遊する。いか釣
り漁船はこの群れを追って、１年を通して水
揚げしている。夜の海原に浮かぶ幻想的な漁
火は、いか釣り漁船の集魚灯のことが多い。
日本では古くから祝い事にするめ（多くはス
ルメイカの乾燥品）を贈る習慣がある。

Japanese common squid migrating in the
sea near Japan is divided into three groups;
ones born in winter, autumn and summer.
Squid-fishing vessels land in chase of it all
year round. Dreamy fishing lights burning
over the ocean at night are almost ones of
squid-fishing vessels. Surume , a dried one,
has been used for a celebratory gift.

鯣烏賊

胴（頭）の長さは
30センチに達し、
背にたての黒帯が見える。

The length of the body reaches
30 cm and a black line can be
seen on its back.

It can be caught somewhere all year round and each cooking method is handed down in each habitat.

1年中どこかしらで獲られ産地それぞれの料理法が伝わる

分類 ツツイカ目アカイカ科　**旬** 6～11月　**料理** 刺身、寿司、いかめし、煮もの、焼きもの、和えもの　**Class:** Teuthida, Ommastrephidae, Todarodes　**Season:** June-November　**Dish:** Sashimi, Sushi, Sticky rice-stuffed squid, Boiled, Grilled, Dressed

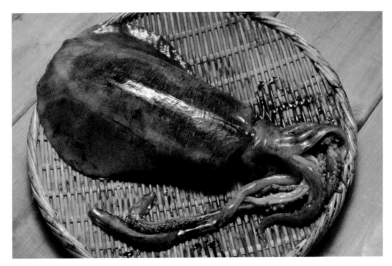

胴の長さ50センチ以上、重さ2キロを超える大型がめずらしくない。胴の周囲にヒレ（耳）を持ち、それをあおって泳ぐことからアオリイカの標準和名がある。イカの仲間ではトップクラスの食味と評される。まとわりつくような食感と強い甘みは、ほかのイカにないものだ。いか墨をよく使う沖縄料理では、アオリイカのそれを珍重する。

The large one over 50 cm in length of the body and 2 kg in weight are very common. Aori ika is the Japanese standard name, named after how to swim fanning with a fin around the body. It has a clinging texture and a strong sweetness, the taste of it is rated highest of squids with such a taste. The ink of squid is made much of in Okinawa because there are many local dishes cooked with it there.

BIGFIN REEF SQUID
アオリイカ

AORIIKA

障泥烏賊

| 分類 ツツイカ目ジンドウイカ科 旬 4～8月 料理 刺身、寿司、てんぷら、くろみ（墨和え） | Class:Myopsida, Loliginidae, Sepioteuthis |

Season:April-August Dish:Sashimi, Sushi, Tempra, Dressed with squid ink

SPEAR SQUID
ヤリイカ

槍烏賊

刺身はこりこりとした食感にすぐれ、あっさりした味わいを持つ。体内に卵を持つメスは「子持ちいか」と別名で呼ばれる。これを煮つければ、ほかにはないむっちりとした歯ざわりと複雑艶麗な味わいを堪能できる。

A slice of it is excellent at a crunchy texture and a plain taste. When you eat boiled female with eggs, also called "Komochi ika", you can enjoy the well-fleshed texture and the complicated rich taste.

分類 ツツイカ目ジンドウイカ科 **旬** 12〜3月 **料理** 糸造り、丸煮、酢のもの **Class:** Myopsida, Loliginidae, Heterololigo
Season: December-March **Dish:** Thin strips , Boiled whole, Vinegared

SWORDTIP SQUID
ケンサキイカ

剣先烏賊

刺身をほおばれば繊細微妙な食感と甘みに、誰もがほれぼれする。全国に名がとどろく呼子(佐賀県唐津市)のいか活き造りは、主にこの種類を使う。生け簀に泳いでいるのをすくいだし、さっとつくるのだからうまいわけだ。

Everybody cannot look upon its delicate texture and sweetness when cramming it. Ones from restaurant's fish-tank is mainly used for Iki-zukuri of Yobuko (Karatsu City, Saga), the famous sashimi dish.

分類 ツツイカ目ジンドウイカ科 **旬** 6〜7月 **料理** 活き造り、寿司、てんぷら、塩焼き、するめ **Class:** Myopsida, Loliginidae, Uroteuthis
Season: June-July **Dish:** Slices of flesh having been cut and put back in place, Sushi, Tempra, Grilled with salt, Dried

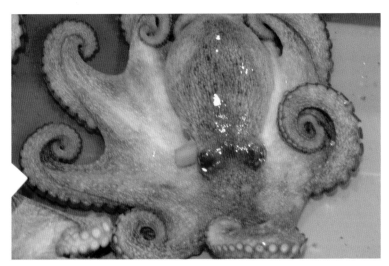

ほかの多くの魚介類が防備のためのウロコや殻を持っている。タコにはそれがない。むきだしの体だから、天敵のタイやウツボの鋭い歯でやられたらひとたまりもない。そのためタコはやたら用心深い。昼間は岩のあいだにかくれ、夜になると長い腕で餌のエビやカニなどをからめとる。伝統の蛸壺漁法では、タコが絶好のかくれ家と思って蛸壺にひそんでいるところを捕獲する。

Octopus doesn't have a shell or scales which many other seafood do for the purpose of defense. If natural predators such as sea bream and moray bite its uncovered body with incisive teeth, it doesn't last two seconds so it is always watchful. In daylight, it hides among rocks. In night, it catches shrimps and crabs with long ltentacles. Fishermen catch it by a traditional octopus fishery with trap pots "Takotsubo" which is good to hide for it.

OCTOPUS
マダコ

MADAKO

分類 八腕形目マダコ科 **旬** 7〜8月、12〜2月 **料理** ゆでだこ、おでん、寿司、煮だこ、干しだこ、たこ飯 **Class:**Octopoda, Octopodidae **Season:**July-August, December-February **Dish:**Boiled, Oden, Sushi, Simmered, Dried, Seasoned and cooked rice with octopus

われわれが食卓でよく見るタコはマダコと
ミズダコ。2種類は単に「タコ」と呼ばれて
混同されがちだが、ちがいがいくつかある。
マダコは東北以南で多く水揚げされ、ミズ
ダコは北海道や三陸が主産地になる。マダ
コは大きくても全長60センチ前後だが、ミ
ズダコは3メートル、体重20キロに達する。
マダコは足がおいしく、ミズダコは胴（頭と
呼ばれる）も足も味がよい。

Octopus, which is often seen at a dining table,
is common octopus and north pacific giant octopus. They are confused because both of
them is simply called "Tako" but they have
some differences. First, the former is mostly
landed in the south of Tohoku and the latter is
mainly landed in Hokkaido and Sanriku. Sec-
ondly, the length of the former is at most 60
cm but the latter reaches 3 m in length and 20
kg in weight. Finally, the legs of the former are
delicious while the delicious parts of the latter
are not only legs but also the body (called a
head).

NORTH PACIFIC GIANT OCTOPUS
MIZUDAKO
水蛸
ミズダコ

分類 八腕形目マダコ科　旬 10～3月　料理 刺身、寿司、酢だこ、干しだこ　Class:Octopoda, Octopodidae　Season:October-March
Dish:Sashimi, Sushi, Vinegaered, Dried

SCALLOP
ホタテガイ

流通する多くが養殖か地撒き放流で
育てられたものだ。養殖方法には二
通りある。一つは籠網の中で稚貝か
ら出荷サイズまで育てる。もう一つ
は籠網で中間育成した貝の殻に穴を
開け、そこに糸を通して海中に垂下
して育てる。地撒き放流では中間育
成した貝を一定の海域に放流し、多
くは3年後に漁獲する。養殖ものは
甘味が強く、地撒き放流ものはこ
りっとした食感にすぐれる。

Most scallop buyable on the market is
cultured, or raised and released. Ones
cultured in net cage have a strong,
sweet taste and ones caught after 3
years of releasing is excellent at the
crunchy texture.

(!) 殻の表には放射状にのびる
20数本の凹凸がある。

There are more than twenty ridges
radially on the uneven surface of
the shell.

(!) 貝柱のまわりに「ヒモ」があり、
産地では食用にされる。

The mantle around the adductor is
eaten in the place of origin.

HOTATEGAI

帆立貝

大きな貝柱を持ち、
この働きで海水を吹き出して
上手に泳ぐ。

It can swim well blowing the
seawater with a large adductor
muscle

You can enjoy
two different tastes
of cultured and
released scallops

養殖ものと地撒き放流ものとがあり
それぞれの味わいを持つ

分類 翼形目イタヤガイ科　旬 11〜5月　料理 刺身、寿司、殻焼き、かき揚げ　**Class:**Pectinoida, Pectinidae **Season:**November-May
Dish: Sashimi, Sushi, Grilled with the shell, Fritter

ABALONE
アワビ

鮑

流通するアワビはマダカアワビ、メガイアワビ、クロアワビ、エゾアワビの4種類。東北以北はエゾアワビ、房総半島以南はクロアワビが多く水揚げされる。どちらもこりこりと歯ごたえがよく、寿司だねによく使われる。

You can buy four types of abalone on the market; Giant abalone, Disk abalone, Japanese abalone and Ezo abalone. They are all crunchy and usually used for sushi topping.

分類 原始腹足目ミミガイ科 **旬** 6 ～ 7月 **料理** 刺身、寿司、地獄焼き、バター焼き、水貝 **Class:** Archaeogastropoda, Haliotidae **Season:** June-July **Dish:** Sashimi, Sushi, Grilled on an ope fire, Grilled with butter, Sliced abalone served in cold water

HARD CLAM
ハマグリ

蛤

かつては内湾性のハマグリが多く漁獲された。これが激減し、今では外洋性の標準和名「チョウセンハマグリ」が「ハマグリ」の名で多く流通している。内湾性より二まわりほど大ぶりで、豊潤なコクをたっぷりと味わえる。

Hard cram with rich taste recently seen in the market is almost pelagic. It is bigger than ones caught in the inner bay and has a rich taste.

分類 異歯目マルスダレガイ科 **旬** 3 ～ 5月 **料理** 潮汁、焼きはまぐり、寿司、ぬた **Class:** Veneridae, Meretrix **Season:** March-May **Dish:** Thin soup, Grilled, Sushi, Salad with vinegar and miso

BLOODY CLAM
アカガイ

赤貝

身があざやかな赤色なのは、血にヘモグロビンが含まれているからだ。魚市場では近似種のサトウガイと区別するためアカガイをホンダマ(本玉)、サトウガイをバッチ(場違い)と呼び分ける。ホンダマがうまい。

Its bright red color of the flesh is made of hemoglobin. In the fish market, it is called "Hondama" against Satogai "Bacchi". Hondama is more delicious.

分類 多歯目フネガイ科　**旬** 10〜3月　**料理** 刺身、寿司、酢のもの　**Class:**Arcida, Arcidae　**Season:**October-March　**Dish:**Sashimi, Sushi, Vinegared

---

OYSTER
カキ

牡蠣

日本近海に約25種あり、われわれが食べているのはマガキという種類。ほとんどが養殖されたものだ。カキ養殖は古くローマ時代の紀元前1世紀のナポリに始まったとされる。日本では1673年に広島県でスタートした。

There are 25 kinds of oyster and we often eat cultured Pacific oysters. Its farming started in Naples in the first century B.C. In Japan, it started in Hiroshima prefecture in 1673.

分類 翼形目イタボガキ科　**旬** 10〜1月　**料理** 酢がき、殻やき、フライ、鍋、かき飯　**Class:**Pteriomorphia, Ostreidae　**Season:**October-January　**Dish:**Vinegared, Grilled with the shell, Fried, Hot pot, Flavored and cooked rice

JAPANESE LITTLENECK CLAM
アサリ

浅蜊

アサリの殻には不規則な山形の紋様がある。ただし北海道産には紋様がほとんどない。殻付きアサリを求めたら必ず砂出しすること。ひたひたの真水に入れ、薄暗く静かな場所に2～3時間おくと砂を吐き出す。

This clam has random chevron patterns on its shell. Flushing the sand out of clams when you buy shelled clam.

分類 異歯目マルスダレガイ科 **旬** 3～6月 **料理** 酒蒸し、吸いもの、味噌汁、あさりご飯　**Class:**Bivalvia, Veneridae **Season:**March-June
Dish: Steamed with sake, Soup, Miso soup, Flavored and cooked rice

---

BASKET CLAM
シジミ

蜆

わが国で食用にされるのはヤマトシジミ、マシジミ、セタシジミの3種類。もっとも多く流通するヤマトシジミは、海水がはいりこむ湖や潟、河川に多く生息する。青森県の十三湖産があふれる滋味で評判を呼んでいる。

Japanese eat three kinds of it; Brackish water clam which is mostly distributed, Asian clam and Seta clam.

分類 異歯目シジミ科 **旬** 4～9月 **料理** 味噌汁、酒蒸し、しじみラーメン　**Class:**Bivalvia, Cyrenidae **Season:**April-September **Dish:**Miso soup, Steamed with sake, Ramen with clam broth

SEA URCHIN
ウニ

海胆

われわれが味わっている国産ウニは、多くがムラサキウニ、アカウニ、バフンウニ、キタムラサキウニ、エゾバフンウニの5種類。東京圏では北海道産のキタムラサキウニが多く流通する。なお食する部分はウニの生殖巣だ。

There are five kinds of Japanese sea urchin. Many of them distributed in the Tokyo metropolitan area are Northern sea urchin caught in Hokkaido. An edible portion of it is gonad.

分類 ホンウニ目オオバフンウニ科 (キタムラサキウニ) 旬 6 ～ 9月 料理 生うに、寿司、いちご煮、うに丼 **Class:**Camarodonta, Strongylocentrotidae(Northern sea urchin) **Season:**June September **Dish:**Raw, Sushi, Boiled with strawberries, Sea urchin rice bowl

SALMON ROE
イクラ

鮭卵

イクラとはサケやマスの卵嚢から成熟卵を一つずつ分けて作った塩蔵品か、醤油漬けのこと。多くがシロザケの魚卵を使う。かめばぷちっとはじける食感のあとにまったりとした旨味が口中に広がる、その具合が好まれる。

"Ikura" means mature eggs of salmon and trout soaked in salt or soy sauce. You can appreciate its popping texture with a bite and then mellow texture and an umami flavor that spreads in the mouth.

旬 9 ～ 11月 料理 寿司、いくら丼 **Season:**September-November **Dish:**Sushi, Salmon roe rice bowl

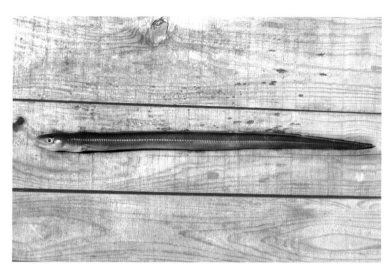

黒潮を南下して産卵するが、どこでふ化してどう成長するかの生態が
わかっていない。春になると太平洋岸各地に10センチ前後の稚魚がや
ってくる。高知県ではこれを「ノレソレ」と呼び、酒の肴として珍重
する。アナゴ漁は多くがアナゴ筒（どう）による。長さ1メートル、直
径20センチ前後の筒を多数つないで海底に流し、餌に誘われてはいっ
てきたアナゴを漁獲する。

This fish goes south to spawn, but where to hatch and grow hasn't been
unexplained in detail. In spring, the young fish comes to the coasts of the
Pacific Ocean. It is called "Noresore" in Kochi prefecture, tasted as a side
dish when drinking liquor. In the case of eel-fishing, fishermen join pipes
around 20 cm in diameter and put them onto the bottom of the sea to
catch eels.

SEA EEL

ANAGO

アナゴ

穴子

分類 ウナギ目アナゴ科クロアナゴ属　**旬** 6～8月　**料理** 蒲焼き、てんぷら、茶碗蒸し、あなごずし　**Class:** Anguilliformes, Congridae.
Conger **Season:** June-August **Dish:** Glaze-grilled, Tempra, A custard-like egg and vegetable dish steamed in a cup, Rod-shaped sushi

JAPANESE FISH MAKET

魚市場を知る

The sketch of

魚市場見取り図

❶ Large fish live box
大型いけす

生きている魚を保管しておく
場所。昼間に届けられた魚は
大型いけすに放たれる。

The cage to keep living fish.
Fishes delivered during the day-
time are released here.

❷ Garbage disposal area
ごみ置き場

市場で出るごみを収集する場
所。発泡スチールなどの資源
ごみはここで分別される。

The area to take out the trash
of the market. Recyclable trash
is separated here.

❸ Intermediate wholesale area
仲卸売り場

仲卸業者が仕入れた魚を売る
場所。買出し人はこの場所で
魚を仕入れる。

Intermediate wholesalers sell
seafood to authorized buyers in
this space.machines at the en-
trance where you order your
food.

❹ Ice-manufactory
製氷所

鮮魚を冷やすための氷を作る
場所。魚を買い付けた人はこ
こで氷を好きなだけ購入可能。

The fish buyers can buy ice to
cool fresh fish here as much as
they like.

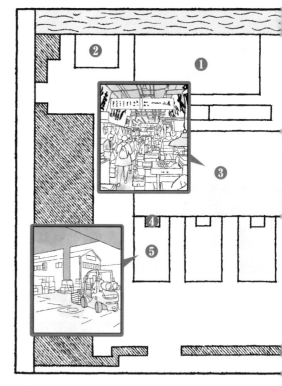

❺ Merchandise storage center
買荷保管所

卸業者が購入した品を保管し
ておく場所。様々な商品がこ
こに保管されている。

A temporary storage for venders
to keep various merchandise.

the fish market

❻ Tuna action area
マグロのせり場

マグロの値段を決める、せり
をするための場所。全てのマ
グロ価格が決定する。

The place to hold tuna auctions.
The prices of tuna is all fixed
here.

❼ Sanitation inspection station
衛生検査所

商品に有害な物質が含まれて
いないかを調べる場所。専用
の機械が設置されている。

The place to identify harmful or
bad products by the specialized
machines.

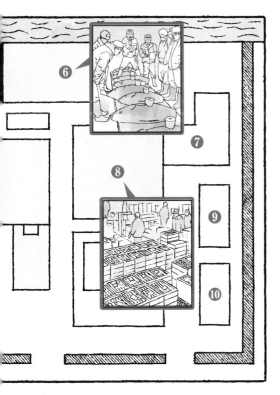

❽ Wholesale area
卸売り場

卸売業が集めた魚を販売する
場所。仲卸業者はここで仕入
れを行う。

The place where wholesalers
sell fish and seafood to intermediate wholesalers.

❾ Refrigerating warehouse
冷凍倉庫

魚介類を冷凍保存しておく場
所。冷凍魚や加工品は-25度、
冷凍マグロは-50度で保管。

The freezer to keep seafood,
storing fish and processed
goods at -25 , tuna at -50 .

❿ Workbench
作業台

魚をさばくための場所。車の
移動販売の運転手はこの場所
で魚をさばく。

The tables to cut a fish. The driv-
ers of mobile wagon dress fishery product here.

魚市場の１日

1 Fishes are collected in the market

魚が市場に集まる

捕獲された魚介類は鮮度を保つため急速に冷却・冷凍され、港に水揚げされる。水揚げされた水産物の多くは、東京の市場へ出荷される。築地市場へは、全国のみならず海外からも、産地・規格・価格などの異なる多種多様な商品が集まる。到着した品物は「卸売業者」が受け取り、品物の状態を見ながら売りやすいようにせり場に並べられていく。

The caught seafood is cooled or frozen quickly before landing at the port to keep freshness. Most of them are landed and transported to the market in Tokyo. The wide variety of products, which are different in production district, size, price and so on, are gathered to Tsukiji Market from not only all parts of Japan and also overseas. "Wholesalers" receive products and place them on the auction area in an easy order to sell according to their condition.

fish market

2 Preparation for the auction and the deal

せり・取引の準備

卸売業者の売り場に「仲卸業者」や「売買
参加者」と呼ばれる人々が集まり、せりの
準備が始まる。マグロはせり場に並べられ
る。販売される魚は、鮮度を保つため、魚
の血を抜く「活き締め」という手法がとら
れる場合もある。仲卸業者、売買参加者は
品物を丹念に下見。大きさや品質、鮮度な
どを厳しくチェックし、あらかじめ買いた
い品物を選び、いくらぐらいで買おうかを
決めて、これから始まるせりに備える。

Venders who are called "intermediate wholesalers" and "authorized buyers" gather in the
wholesale area and start to prepare for the
auction. The wholesaler place tuna on the
auction area. Some fish are deblooded to
keep freshness, which is the method called
"Ikishime". Intermediate wholesalers and authorized buyers look over products and sup-
plies prior to auction. They thoroughly check
the size, quality, freshness and so on, and
then they decide which and you much to buy
before the auction.

A day of the

魚市場の１日

3 Start of the auction

せり・取引

水産物のせりは朝５時頃から開始。鐘の音を合図にせりが始まると、売り手であるせり人の呼び掛けに応じて仲卸業者、売買参加者が指で値段を示していく。一番高い値段をつけた人がその魚を買うことができる。せり人は多くの買い手の中から、一番高い値段を示した買い手の名前を読み上げて競り落とす。せりは売り場を移動しながら行われ、次々に買い手が決まっていく。

The tuna auction starts about 5 a.m. with the sound of the bell as a start signal. Responding to a call of an auctioneer, intermediate wholesalers and authorized buyers show the price they are hoping for by fingers. The auctioneer calls the name of the highest bidders of many buyers and knock the product down. The auction is held while changing the counter. As it takes only a few seconds to sell one tuna, one action is finished after another.

064

fish market

4 Packing and delivering fish

箱詰め・出荷

仲卸業者は、せりで仕入れた商品を順次仲卸売場にある自分の店舗に運ぶ。必要に応じて、加工や小分けをして売場に並べ、買い出しに来た小売業の客に販売する。買われた商品は、待機していたトラックに積まれて量販店や小売店へ向う。卸売場や仲卸売場では、商品が運び出された後は、後片づけや清掃が行われる。卸売業者は出荷者と連絡をとって本日の売り報告と翌日売りの準備を行う。

The intermediate wholesalers send products in order to their shops in the intermediate wholesalers area. After processing their products or dividing them to the appropriate size as needed, they place their goods on the counter and sell to retail dealers. The retail dealers send purchases to supermarkets and retail shops by truck. After the products are delivered out, the wholesale area and the intermediate wholesaler area are cleaned up. The wholesalers receive the selling report from the stock purchasers and prepare for the deal of the next day.

The manners of the market tour

市場を見学する時のマナー

---

(1) **Check a website beforehand because how to observe varies with the market.**

見学の方法は市場ごとに異なるので、事前に必ずホームページなどを確認する。

(2) **Don't touch seafood which is for sale.**

取引されている魚介類には触らない。

(3) **Refrain from going with many companions or bringing a big baggage not to bother the market venders.**

市場で働く人々や交通に支障が出ないように、大人数での行動や大きな荷物の持ち込みはひかえる。

(4) **Don't enter the market with wobbly shoes such as heel shoes or sandals because some area is slippy with water in the market.**

場内は水に濡れていて滑りやすい場所もある。ヒールやサンダルなど、不安定な履物で入場しない。

(5) **No Smoking. It prohibits the bringing dangerous goods or pets.**

原則禁煙。危険物の持ち込み、動物を連れての入場はできない。

(6) **There are some areas where flash photography or photography itself is prohibited.**

フラッシュ撮影が禁止の区域、写真撮影自体が禁止の区域もある。

(7) **It is not impossible for general visitors to buy seafood from an intermediary agent, but you have to buy over a definite amount. You cannot buy only one fish.**

一般人も仲介業者から魚介類を購入することは不可能ではない。ただし、一定の単位以上の購入が必要で、1尾買いは厳禁。

(8) **Never beat the price down when you buy seafood from an intermediary agent.**

仲介業者から魚介類を購入するときは、決して値切らない。

Canned food in Japan

日本の缶詰

くだものやスープ等、世の中にはたくさんの缶詰があるが、日本で多く製造されているのは魚の缶詰だ。水煮、味噌煮以外にも、蒲焼きやカニみそ、本格的なおつまみまである。もともと缶詰は、1800年代初頭にナポレオンが遠征時の食料補給問題を解決するため開発させたのがはじまりといわれている。日本に缶詰が伝わったのは1870年頃だが、一般家庭に普及したのは関東大震災以降。魚の缶詰は、塩分が多いものの、長期保存に向き、栄養価が高く、骨まで食べられる点に優れている。最近では、その高いクオリティーを活かした缶詰バーが存在する。

Though there are various kinds of canned food in the world such as fruits and soup, the canned food which is mostly made in Japan is that of fish. In Japan, you can choose one from many kinds of it — fish which is boiled, simmered with miso, grilled with soy sauce, crab innards, high-quality nibbles and so on. The origin is said to be early in the 1800s, when Napoleon commanded to develop it in order to solve the problem of military provisions supply. It was introduced into Japan in the 1870s and had spread to an ordinary home after the Great Kanto Earthquake. Canned fish is salty but good for long term preservation and very nutritious. In addition, even the bones of it are eatable. Lately, the canned food bar that makes the most of the high quality of it appeared.

FISHING PORT AND MARKET

日本の漁港・市場

FISHING PORTS
AND MARKETS IN JAPAN

日本の漁港と市場

　日本の漁港は実に3000近くを数え、そこから大小の漁船が毎日のように出漁している。大半は1〜2名が乗り込む3トン未満だが、大型まき網漁船やマグロ延縄漁船、大型トロール漁船といった大型漁船も、はるか沖合いで操業している。漁船はとった魚を漁港に水揚げして、せりや入札にかける。魚はそこから流通が始まってようやく消費者の食卓に届く。一方「朝市」と呼ばれる産地直売の市場がある。多くは漁港で開かれ、鮮度のいいうちに魚を販売する。だから地元の主婦やプロの料理人が足繁く通うほか、魚好きや観光客が遠くからわざわざ足を運ぶ。

There are nearly 3000 fish ports in Japan, and large or small fishing vessels go fishing from them almost daily. Most of them are less than 3 tons in weight with one or two fishermen on board. Large vessels such as large round haul netters, tuna long liners and large trawlers also operate far off the coat. After fishing, they land and sell seafoods they caught at ports. Distribution starts from here and they are delivered to consumers' tables, taking some steps. On the other hand, at "Asaichi", the fish market directly sold to for general consumers held near a fishing port, you can buy seafoods while they are fresh. Other than local housewives and professional chefs visit there frequently and, fish lovers and tourists come all the way from far.

Map of fishingports and markets in Japan

全国の漁港・市場マップ

HIROME ICHIBA

ひろめ市場　⇒**P.092**

KARATO ICHIBA

唐戸市場　⇒**P.090**

YOBUKO ASAICHI

呼子朝市　⇒**P.094**

MAKISHI PUBRIC MARKET

牧志公設市場　⇒**P.096**

浜田／HAMADA

長崎／NAGASAKI

枕崎／MAKURAZAKI

NIJO ICHIBA
二条市場　⇒**P.074**

OMI-CHO ICHIBA
近江町市場　⇒**P.084**

HAKODATE ASAICHI
函館朝市　⇒**P.076**

釧路／KUSHIRO

AKITA SHIMIN ICHIBA
秋田市民市場　⇒**P.078**

石巻／ISHINOMAKI

境港／SAKAIMINATO

NAKAMINATO OSAKANA ICHIBA
那珂湊おさかな市場　⇒**P.080**

築地／TSUKIJI

銚子／CHOSHI

YAIZU SAKANA CENTER
焼津さかなセンター　⇒**P.082**

土佐清水／TOSASHIMIZU

KUROMON ICHIBA
黒門市場　⇒**P.086**

UO-NO-TANA
魚の棚　⇒**P.088**

SAPPORO

二条市場/NIJO ICHIBA

明治時代初期に石狩浜の漁師がここで魚を売ったのが始まりと伝わる。一世紀半をへた今も西1丁目から東2丁目にかけて鮮魚店がずらりと並び、豊富な北の幸と売り手のかけ声が買い物気分を誘っている。観光客にはタラバガニとケガニが人気だ。大通公園から徒歩5分と足を向けやすい。

Early years of the Meiji here era when fishermen from Ishikari Beach sold fishes is considered to be the beginning of this market. Nowadays, after a century and one half, fresh fish shops line both sides of the streets from Nishi 1-chome to Higashi 1-chome. Snow crab and hairy crab are popular with tourists. It is easily accessible of 5 minutes by foot from Odori park.

〒060-0053　北海道札幌市中央区南2条東1丁目
☎ 011-222-5308　URL http://nijomarket.com/
Add: Higashi 1 chome Minami 2-jyo, Chuo-ku, Sapporo, Hokkaido
060-0053 Tel: 011-222-5308　URL: http://nijomarket.com/

観光客はカニ類のほか、新巻や
イクラなどのおみやげ選びに余
念がない。買い物のあとは北の
幸満載の海鮮丼をほおばるのが
定番コース。周辺には「のれん
横町」などの飲食店が数多くあ
って、人気スポットになってい
る。

Tourists put their hearts into
choosing souvenirs — crabs,
salmon called Aramaki, salmon
raw and so on. It is the classic
plan to enjoy eating fresh seafood
bowl after shopping. The market
area, including "Noren Yokocho",
is known as a foodie destination
with many restaurants.

秋の二条市場はサケが主役にな
る。多くは半身や切り身で並ぶ
が、地元の人は1尾を買い求め
て丸ごとむだにせずに石狩鍋に
する。春から夏にかけて水揚げ
されるサケ「トキシラズ」は、
産卵に間があるため脂がよくの
り味に定評がある。

Autumn is the season of salmon
in the Nijo Ichiba. Local people
buy it whole and use the head and
bony parts without any waste to
Ishikari Nabe, which is a Hokkaido
specialty, a salmon hot pot with
miso. "Tokishirazu", a salmon
which is landed from spring
through summer, is noted for its
fattiness.

ARAMAKI
アラマキ

新巻

大半のサケ（標準和名シロザケ）は秋に漁獲されることから、北海道では
「秋あじ」と呼ばれる。その多くは産地で新巻や塩ざけに加工されて消費地
へ運ばれる。新巻のなかでも浜の潮風でじっくりと干し上げた「寒風干し」
が食通たちをうならせる。

In Hokkaido, it is referred to as "Akiaji" which means the food of autumn, since
salmon is mainly caught in autumn. Most of it are preserved with salt and de-
liverd as Aramaki and Siozake. Among Aramaki, "Kanpu-boshi" which is well
dried in the sea-breeze especially makes a deep impression to gourmets.

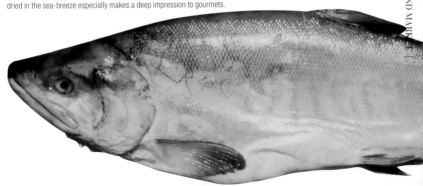

HAKODATE

函館朝市/HAKODATE ASAICHI

函館は北海道有数の観光都市。函館はまた広い海岸線を持つ海の幸の宝庫でもあり、函館市水産物地方卸売市場では毎朝多種多様な近海ものがせりにかけられている。函館朝市は函館駅のすぐ南側に隣接しており、交通の便がよい。列車待ちのあいだにふらっと立ち寄る観光客もいて、いつも朝早くから買い物客で賑わっている。

Hakodate is one of popular sightseeing cities in Hokkaido. It has a long coastline where a lot of seafood is caught. A wide variety of shorefish are sold by action every morning in the Hakodate wholesale market of fisheries products. Hakodate morning market has best access to transportation, adjoining on the south of Hakodate station. Some tourists stop by while waiting for the train and the market is always crowded with many people from early morning.

〒040-0063　北海道函館市若松町9-19
0120-858-313　URL http://www.hakodate-asaichi.com/
Add: 9-10 Wakamatsu-cho, Hakodate, Hokkaido 040-0063
Tel:0120-858-313 URL: http://www.hakodate-asaichi.com/

早朝の函館市水産物地方卸売市場でせり落とされた鮮魚は、ただちに朝市へ。だからここの魚は活きがいい。新巻、数の子、筋子、タラコ、するめ、函館特産のがごめ昆布といった加工品の種類も多く、格好のおみやげになっている。

The seafood bought in the early morning at the Hakodate wholesale fish market is delivered to the morning market in a minute. Many processed marine products which are the specialty of Hakodate are bought for souvenirs — Aramaki, herring roe, salted salmon roe, cod roe, dried squid, Kagome kelp and so on.

朝市でおみやげを買い込んだら、次はいかそうめんを食べたくなる。函館名物のこの料理では、6月から翌年1月にかけてはスルメイカ、5〜6月にはヤリイカが使われる。歯ざわりのよさとするりとしたのどごしが楽しい。

After buying souvenirs in the morning market, let's slurp Ika Somen, a shredded sashimi of squid. It is made of a Japanese flying squid from June to January, spear squid in May and June. Both of them are excellent in touch feeling to the teeth and tongue, smoothness to the throat.

HAIRY CRAB
ケガニ

KEGANI

函館朝市のケガニは活けやゆで、ボイル冷凍で並ぶ。活けをゆでて熱いうちにしゃぶるのが一番。冷凍ものは冷蔵庫内でゆっくり自然解凍するか、塩を加えた熱湯で2〜3分ゆでなおすとうまい。

In the Hakodate morning market, hair crab is sold living, being boiled or boiled-and-cold. The best way to taste it is to boil a live crab and chew on it while hot. If frozen, it is better to defrost naturally in the refrigerator or re-boiled in hot water with salt for 2-3 minutes.

AKITA

秋田市民市場／AKITA SHIMIN ICHIBA

秋田市は秋田県の沿岸中部に位置し、北にハタハタで知られる八森漁港（八峰町）、南にタラ漁が盛んな金浦漁港（にかほ市）やイワガキが水揚げされる象潟漁港（同）などがある。日本海の荒波でもまれて育った魚介は、鮮度のいいままに秋田市民市場へ運ばれる。ここは地元の主婦が多く「市民の台所」といわれる。

Akita city is located in the middle of the coast of Akita Prefecture. There are some famous fishing ports; for example, Hachimori, which is known for sandfish, is on the north side of the city (Happo-cho). Konoura, where cod fishery thrives, and Kisakata, where Iwagaki oyster is landed, are on the south side (Nikaho city). The seafood tossed about by heavy Japanese sea is delivered to Akita Shimin Ichiba while it is fresh. This market is referred to as the "Kitchen of Akita" because local people usually go to purchase ingredients there.

所 〒010-0001　秋田県秋田市中通4-7-35
☎ 018-833-1855　URL http://www.akitashiminichiba.com/
Add: 4-7-35 Nakadori, Akita-shi, Akita-ken 010-0001
Tel: 018-833-1855　URL: http://www.akitashiminichiba.com/

館内に鮮魚や青果など200軒近くの店が
並ぶ。鮮魚店には主婦にまじって料理
人の姿が目立つ。プロが認めるほど新
鮮な魚を並べているのだ。ＪＲ秋田駅
から徒歩5分と交通の便がよく、観光客
がぶらりと立ち寄っている。

The market is lined with no less than 200
fish dealers and greengrocers. There are
some professional chefs in the crowds of
customers for fresh seafood. It is well located within a 5-minute walk from the JR
Akita Station and tourists stop over there.

COD
タラ

TARA

標準和名はマダラ。北海道や青森県、秋田県に多く水揚げされる。
タラの産地として古くから知られる金浦では、底引き網で漁獲す
る。秋田の人たちはあらや肝を利用するじゃっぱ汁や焼きもの、
白子ポン酢和えで味わうことが多い。旬は12〜1月。

The Japanese standard name is Madara. Most of are is landed on Akita Prefecture. Fishermen in Konoura fishing port, where has long been
known for cod fishery, use a trawl net to catch it. The citizens of Akita
generally taste it as Jappa-jiru, the soup made with bony parts and liver of it, grilled one and its soft roe with ponzu sauce. The best season
is from December to January.

SAILFIN SANDFISH
ハタハタ

HATAHATA

「秋田名物八森はたはた男鹿で
男鹿ぶりこ」と秋田音頭にうた
われる通り、男鹿半島の漁港
や八森漁港にはハタハタが多
く水揚げされる。秋田の漁師
は産卵で浅場にやってきたと
ころを刺し網で漁獲する。旬
は12〜1月。

Many sandfish is landed on fishing ports of the Oga Peninsula
and the Hachimori fishing port,
as a line in the Akita Ondo (folk
song). Fishermen of Akita catch
this fish with the gill nets when it
comes to a shallow area to lay
eggs. The best season is from
December to January.

NAKAMINATO

那珂湊おさかな市場/NAKAMINATO OSAKANA ICHIBA

沿岸漁業と沖合い漁業の漁船が、那珂湊漁港に多種類の魚介を水揚げする。那珂湊おさかな市場は漁港の敷地内にあり、毎朝4時からのセリで落とされたばかりの魚がすばやく運ばれる。東京から鉄道で2時間ほどと近く、多くの魚好きたちが足繁く通ってくる。ひたちなか海浜鉄道那珂湊駅から徒歩12分。

There are coastal and offshore fishery vessels in the Nakaminato fishing port and many types of seafood is landed there. Nakaminato Osakana Ichiba is located in such a market and fishes are bought by actions from 4 o'clock every morning and delivered immediately. It is just 2 hours by train and relatively close to the metropolitan area and many people who loves seafood visit there frequently. 12 minutes' walk from Hitachinaka Seaside Railway Nakaminato Station.

所 〒311-1221　茨城県ひたちなか市湊本町19-8
電 029-263-6779　URL http://www.nakaminato-osakanaichiba.jp/
Add: 19-8 Minatohoncho, Hitachinaka, Ibaraki 311-1221
Tel: 029-263-6779　URL: http://www.nakaminato-osakanaichiba.jp/

名産のアンコウやドンコのほか、カレイ類、スズキ、タコ、イカ類、ヒラメなどどれも鮮度のよさが自慢の。「常磐もの」というブランド魚で、東京・築地市場での評価が高い。魚を買い求めるとサービスで刺身や切り身にさばいてくれる。

Seafood on the market is all fresh— the specialty such as monkfish and brown hakeling, flatfish, perch, octopus, squid, flounder and so on. They are highly-praised as "Joban-mono" at Tsukiji Market in Tokyo. When you buy some fish, a fish dealer cuts it to a piece or slice for free if you want.

深海魚のドンコ（標準和名エゾイソアイナメ）は見た目はグロテスクだが、白身は淡白で、肝は濃厚で旨味たっぷり。肝焼きや肝味噌たたき、味噌汁とドンコ料理ではいずれも肝が主役になる。冬になると肝が肥大してうまさがぐんと増す。

The Japanese standard name of Brown hakeling is Ezoisoainame. The taste of its white meat is plain, but its liver has a rich taste. When you eat brown hakeling, the liver is the main part of dishes, like grilled liver, miso-based liver tartar and miso soup. In winter, it grows bigger and the taste gets richer.

MONKFISH
アンコウ

ANKOU

鮟鱇

常磐沖には寒流と暖流の交わる絶好の漁場があり、ここで育つ「常磐もの」のアンコウは味のよさで広く知られる。鍋用にさばいたセットを買えば、自宅で簡単に高級あんこう鍋を囲める。旬は11〜3月。

There is a golden fishery between warm and cold sea currents off the coast of Joban. Monkfish of "Joban-mono", which is caught in Joban, is widely known for good taste. You can buy the pack for a hot pot and enjoy high-class Ankou Nabe in your own home. The best season is from November to March.

YAIZU

焼津さかなセンター／YAIZU SAKANA CENTER

焼津漁港にはまき網やマグロ遠洋はえ縄、定置網、一本釣りなどの漁船が、さまざまな魚を大量に水揚げしている。特にマグロ類やカツオ、サバ、コノシロの水揚げ量は全国でもトップクラス。焼津さかなセンターには焼津漁港に水揚げされた魚が豊富に並び、プロの料理人も多く集まる。

Such as round haul netters, tuna long liners, fixed net, ones using fishing net and pole-and-line fishing, many vessels belong and land a catch of a volume of fishes to the Yaizu fishing port. The catches of tuna, bonito, mackerel and dotted gizzard shad are ones of the largest in Japan. The Yaizu Sakana Center has a large selection of fishes landed to the Yaizu fishing port and many professional chefs come visit to the center.

所 〒425-0091　静岡県焼津市八楠4-13-7
☎ 054-628-1137　URL http://www.sakana-center.com/
Add: 4-13-7 Yagusu, Yaizu, Shizuoka 425-0091
Tel: 054-628-1137　URL: http://www.sakana-center.com/

焼津さかなセンターは、広大な
館内に71店舗がそろう。鮮魚店
が地元に水揚げされるマグロ類
やカツオ、ブリなどを並べ、加
工直売店がシラス干しや干しサ
クラエビ、かまぼこなどの特産
品を売る。買い物のあとは大食
堂で魚料理に舌鼓を打ちたい。

There are 71 shops in the extensive building. Fish dealers sell local fishes like tunas, bonitos, yellowtail and so on. Direct sales
stores sell the specialty such as
dried young sardines, dried saku-
ra shrimp and boiled fish-pastes.
You should taste seafood in the
large cafeteria after shopping.

TUNA
マグロ

焼津漁港には遠洋はえ縄漁法で漁獲されたマグロ類が、数多く水揚
げされる。焼津さかなセンターの鮮魚店ではそれを仕入れて包丁を
入れ、多くはさくとして販売する。時期にもよるがクロマグロ、メバ
チ、キハダ、ビンナガとそろう。

In Yaizu fishing port, a lot of tuna caught by deep-sea long liners is landed. The fish dealer of the Yaizu Sakana Center buys and cuts it into blocks
and sells them. Although depending on the season, bluefin tuna, bigeye
tuna, yellowfin tuna and albacore are on sale there.

WHITEBAIT
シラス

シラスとは主にカタクチイワシの稚魚
のことだ。生のほか、釜揚げ、ボイル
して生干ししたしらす干し、よく乾燥
させたちりめん干しなどに加工される。
漁期の焼津さかなセンターでは生しら
すが人気となっている。

Whitebait is almost the young of the sardine. It is sold both raw and processed to
"Kama-age" which is boiled, half-dried,
"Shirasu-boshi" and well dried one.
"Chirimen-boshi" Raw whitebait calls
people to the Yaizu Sakana center in its
best season.

KANAZAWA

近江町市場/OMI-CHO ICHIBA

金沢には鯛の唐蒸しなど加賀料理の数々が伝わる。伝統の食文化を長く支えてきたのが、目前に広がる日本海からの幸だ。近江町市場は加賀藩の御膳所から始まり、今は市民の台所を担う。1年でもっともにぎわうのは12〜2月。ズワイガニやブリ、アマエビ、ナマコなど冬の日本海の美味が人を呼び寄せる。

Such as Tai no Karamushi, the Chinese-style steamed sea bream, a lot of Kaga Cuisine have been passed down in Kanazawa. It goes without saying that seafood of the sea of Japan in front of the city has supported traditional food culture. Omi-cho Ichiba started as the kitchen of Kaga Domains and now plays that of the citizen. The most bustling season is from December to February. The winter delicacies such as snow crab, yellowtail, sweet shrimp and sea cucumber, bring customers there.

所 〒920-0905　石川県金沢市上近江町50
☎ 076-231-1462　URL http://ohmicho-ichiba.com/
Add: 50 kamiomicho, Kanazawa, Ishikawa 920-0905
Tel: 076-231-1462　URL: http://ohmicho-ichiba.com/

広大なアーケード街に鮮魚、青果、乾物、惣菜、飲食などの店舗が170軒あまり。鮮魚店は20店舗を数える。10時を回るとまずプロの料理人が立ち寄る。11時を過ぎると地元の主婦や観光客が加わり一段とにぎわう。

The number of shops in this extensive arcade is over 170, including fish dealers, greengrocers, grocers, delicatessens, restaurants and so on. After ten o'clock, professional chefs visit there at first and then, after eleven o'clock, the market becomes more crowded with local people and tourists.

SNOW CRAB
ズワイガニ

金沢のかに好きたちは活けを買い求め「あらい」で味わう。脚の身を冷水で洗う。するとまるで花が咲いたような形に縮まり、優雅な舌ざわりとおいしさを生み出す。塩焼きは産地でも贅沢な一品だ。

The crab lovers in Kanazawa buy a live crab and taste it by "Arai". Arai is a cooking method to cut off the leg shells and wash it in cold water. This method makes the meat shrink like a flower blooming and it becomes delicious and graceful on the tongue. The salt-grilled one is extravagant even there.

YELLOWTAIL
ブリ

BURI

鰤

金沢にはブランド魚の「能登ぶり」や「氷見ぶり」の産地が比較的近い。寒さ厳しいブリ漁のシーズンを迎えると、活きのいいものが近江町市場の店先に並ぶ。

The locality of Notoburi and Himiburi is relatively near Kanazawa. On the strictly cold season of buri fishing, fresh fishes are sold at Omi-cho Ichiba.

OSAKA

黒門市場/KUROMON ICHIBA

大阪は海の幸に恵まれている。目前に大阪湾が広がり、西には播磨灘が続き、マダイの明石やワタリガニの室津（たつの市）などの水揚げ地が点在する。南の紀伊水道に目を向ければマダイの加太（和歌山市）や鳴門、ハモの椿泊（阿南市）などがある。さらに日本海の魚介が運ばれてくる。黒門市場は豊富な水産物などで「食い倒れの町」を支える。

Osaka is blessed with the bounty of the sea. The city is overlooking the Osaka Bay and continuing to the Harima Bay to the west. There are locations for landing scattered such as Red seabream's Akashi and Blue crab's Murotsu (Tatsuno City). In the Kii Channel, the south, there are Red seabream's Kada (Wakayama Prefecture) and Naruto and Pike conger's Tsubakidomari (Anan city). Moreover, seafoods from the Sea of Japan are transported. Kuromon Ichiba supports the "Town of Kuidaore" with abundant seafoods.

所 〒542-0073　大阪府大阪市中央区日本橋2-4-1
☎ 06-6631-0007　URL http://www.kuromon.com/
Add: 2-4-1 Nipponbashi, Chuo-ku, Osaka-shi, Osaka-fu 542-0073
Tel: 06-6631-0007　URL:http://www.kuromon.com/

黒門市場は食の宝庫。青果、乾物、飲食店とそろう中で、主役は鮮魚店。マグロで勝負する店や調理済みの魚を売る店などが、浪速っ子たちの胃袋を満たす。

Kuromon Ichiba is a treasury of food. There are many shops such as greengrocers, grocers and restaurants, but the main is fish dealers. Some stores compete on tuna and others to sell processed fishes satisfy the robust appetite of a native of Osaka.

文政年間に堺や紀州の漁師が魚を売り始めたのがルーツとされる。今は縦600メートル、横300メートルのアーケード街におよそ180店舗が揃う。売り手の威勢のいい大阪弁が飛び交い、買い手の食欲を誘っている。

The origin is considered that the fishermen of Sakai and Kishu started to sell fishes in the Bunsei era. Now there are about 180 shops. The vigorous Osaka dialect of sellers is flying from all directions, developing a buyer's appetite.

PIKE CONGER
ハモ

ハモ

鱧

旬の夏を迎えると黒門市場にはハモの照り焼きや湯引きがずらりと並ぶ。浪速っ子たちはこの魚のしっとりとしたおいしさを贔屓にする。

In summer, pike congers broiled with soy sauce and parboiled ones are lined up. The moist texture of this fish is in favor of a native of Osaka.

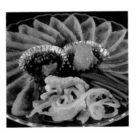

TESSA
テッサ

テッサ

てっさ

大阪の人はフグの刺身を「てっさ」と呼ぶ。当たれば危険なフグの毒を鉄砲にたとえ「鉄砲の刺身」、略して「てっさ」になる。旬は冬。

In Osaka, sashimi of pufferfish is called "Tessa", the shortening of "Teppo-no-Sashimi". People compare its poison to a gun which is dangerous to be hit. The best season is winter.

AKASHI

魚の棚/UO-NO-TANA

明石市は東西16キロにわたって瀬戸内海に接している。目前は明石海峡。ここで漁獲されるマダイは「明石鯛」、マダコは「明石蛸」と呼ばれて、味のよいことで名高い。明石駅から数分歩くと「魚の棚」（地元の人は「うおんたな」と発音する）に到着する。その名の通りに魚が主役のアーケード街だ。

Akashi City is adjacent to the Seto Inland Sea, east and west about 16 kilometers. The Akashi Channel is in the face of it. Red seabream caught in Akashi is called "Akashidai" and common octopus is called "Akashidako", both of them are famous for good taste. It takes a few minutes from Akashi Station to "Uo-no-Tana", pronounced "Uontana" by local people. Just like the name, the star of the arcade is fish.

所 〒673-0892　兵庫県明石市本町1-1-6
☎ 078-911-9666　URL http://www.uonotana.or.jp/
Add: 1-1-6 Honmachi, Akashi, Hyogo 673-0892
Tel: 078-911-9666　URL: http://www.uonotana.or.jp/

「昼網」の札付きからまず売れていく。魚の棚近くにある林崎漁港の漁船は、早朝に出船して昼前のせりに魚をかける。これが昼網の魚だ。カサゴなどの磯魚は飛び跳ねるほど活きがいい。

The vessels of Hayashizaki fishing ports near Uo-no-Tana go fishing early in the morning and sell fishes by auction before noon. These fishes are tagged as "Hirua-mi". Inshore fishes like rockfish are so fresh that they jump.

魚の棚はおよそ400年前の明石城築城とともに生まれ、設計者はかの宮本武蔵と伝わる。今はアーケード街に100軒あまり。そのうち鮮魚店13軒と海産物店が20軒。ここで買い物いっさいを済ませる主婦が少なくない。

Uo-no-Tana was built about 400 years ago when Akashi-Jo Castle was constructed. The architect is said to be that Miyamoto Musashi. Now there are over 100 shops on the arcade. Not a few housewives complete shopping of daily foods there.

OCTOPUS
マダコ

MADAKO

真蛸

「明石蛸」は足が太くて短く「明石のタコは陸で立って歩く」といわれる。エビやカニなど明石海峡の栄養豊かな餌を食べてよく育っており、味のよさは折り紙付き。底引き網と蛸壺漁で漁獲される。

"Akashidako" has thick and short legs and it's said that "octopus of Akashi" stand and walk onshore". It grows fat, eating nutritious feed in the Akashi Channel such as shrimps and crabs. The good taste of it is certified. They are caught with a trawl net or an octopus trap pod.

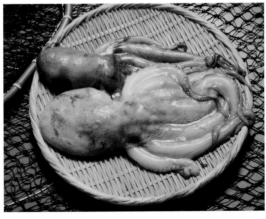

SHIMONOSEKI

唐戸市場/KARATO ICHIBA

下関市は本州西端に位置して瀬戸内海と日本海に面し、近隣に点在する大小の漁港から多くの魚介が集まってくる。なかでもトラフグは全国からここの南風泊市場（えとまり）に送られ、取扱い量は日本一。唐戸市場の同じ館内には地方卸売市場と一般向け市場があり、2階デッキから買い物ついでにせりを見学できる。

Simonoseki City is located at the west end of Honshu and faces the Seto Inland Sea and the Sea of Japan. Many seafood is delivered there from large or small fishing ports scattered in the vicinity. Japanese pufferfish is sent to the Haedomari Ichiba from all over Japan and the amount of its transaction is top of Japan. There are both local wholesale market and market for general consumers in a building. You can observe fish auctions from the second floor deck while shopping.

所 〒750-0005　山口県下関市唐戸町5-50
☎ 083-231-0001　URL http://www.karatoichiba.com/
Add: 5-50 Karatocho, Shimonoseki, Yamaguchi 750-0005
Tel: 083-231-0001　URL: http://www.karatoichiba.com/

館内には女性たちの威勢のいいかけ声「かわんかあ！」が飛び交う。高価な天然トラフグのほか、沿岸や近海で獲れた魚介が棚からこぼれんばかり。毎週末と祝日には飲食イベント「活きいき馬関街」を開催している。

The women woking there shout energetically "Kawankah!". The counters are filled with seafood caught in the coast and the sea near the city, in addition to expensive Japanese pufferfish. The food and drink event called "Ikiiki Bakan-gai" is held on every weekend and holidays.

南風泊市場の仲買人たちは周防灘や伊予灘で育ったトラフグを「内海もの」と呼び、東シナ海や日本海で獲れる「外海もの」と区別する。内海ものは豊富な小エビや貝類を餌にして育ち、身質がよくて高値で取引される。

The brokers of the Haedomari market call Japanese pufferfishes which grew in Suounada and Iyonada "Uchiumi-mono" and ones which grew in the East China Sea and the Sea of Japan "Sotoumimono". The formers are traded at a high price because of good-quality meat.

TIGER PUFFER
トラフグ

TORAFUGU

虎河豚

南風泊市場では独特の「袋ぜり」でトラフグの値を決める。せり人と買い受け人が黒い布袋の中に手を入れて、握った指の本数などで取引。買い受け人は活魚や身がき（頭や皮、内臓を取り除いたもの）で全国へ発送する。

In the Haedomari market, the price of Japanese pufferfish is fixed by Fukurozeri. It is a unique method of auction that a seller and a buyer put their hands into a bag of black cloth and tell a desired price by showing the number on fingers. Buyers sent it as a live fish or Migaki (cleaned fish without head, skin and inner parts) to all over Japan.

KOCHI

ひろめ市場/HIROME ICHIBA

高知には大皿に盛って大人数で囲む皿鉢料理が古くから伝わる。主に盛り込まれる料理は刺身、組みもの、寿司の三皿。高知市や近くの須崎市、さらに中土佐町、黒潮町などの各漁港から送られてきた魚介が皿鉢料理を飾る。ひろめ市場は繁華街にある人気の屋台村。40軒ほどの飲食店で手軽に土佐の味を注文できる。

In Kochi, the big-dish cuisine surrounded and eaten by many people has long been passed down. They are mainly divided into three dishes; assorted sashimi, sushi and an assortment of seafood dishes. Seafood sent from the fishing ports of Kochi, Susaki close by, Nakatosa-cho and Kuroshio-cho, are often used to this cuisine. Hirome is a famous food stall village in the shopping district. You can enjoy the taste of Tosa easily at about 40 restaurants there.

平成浪漫商店街
ひろめ市場

土 ☆ 食
潮 佐 楽

〒780-0841 高知県高知市帯屋町2-3-1
088-822-5287 URL http://hirome.co.jp/
Add: 2-3-1 Obiyamachi, Kochi-shi, Kochi-ken 780-0841
Tel: 088-822-5287 URL: http://hirome.co.jp/

4000平方メートルの館内に種種
雑多な屋台がぎっしり。すべて
セルフサービスで、店は料理を
作って提供するだけ。客は料理
を受け取って館内のテーブルス
ベースでいただく。気安さと個
性きわだつ一皿が多くの人を集
めている。

The market is filled with various
stalls in the building of 4000 meters square. They are all self-ser-
vice restaurants. The staffs cook
food and customers receive and
carry it to eating area. Many people come there for its friendliness
and unique dishes.

正門からはいってすぐ右手の
「黒潮水産」が魚介類をそろえて
いる。漁期になればカツオがメ
イン。さくや刺身、たたき、焼
きがつおがよく売れる。土佐の
人は焼きがつおをそのまま食べ
るだけでなく、野菜炒めなどい
ろいろな料理に利用する。

Kuroshio-suisan fishery sells various seafood on the right just as
you enter the main gate. Bonitos
are the star in the fishing season.
The block, sashimi, roasted bonito
and Namabushi sell very well.
Tosa people eat namabushi in
many ways, not only boiled but
also stir-fried with vegetables.

SKIPJACK TUNA
カツオ

高知の漁船は一本釣り漁でカツオを獲るほか、引き縄漁法で沿岸に寄ってきたカツオを釣
り上げる。漁は小型漁船で行われ、午前2時に出漁して午後2時にカツオを水揚げする。日
帰りで漁をする「日戻りがつお」は、鮮度のよさから高値で取引される。

Other than the fishing vessel of Kochi catches bonitos by pole-and-line fishing, some land ones
approaching the coast with towrope. This small vessel goes fishing at 2 a.m. and land bonitos
at 2 p.m. "Himodori Gatsuo" caught on the same day, traded at a high price because of good
freshness.

YOBUKO

呼子朝市/YOBUKO ASAICHI

唐津市呼子は天然の良港を持ち、目前の玄界灘に好漁場を有し古くから漁師町として栄えてきた。今は数多くのいか釣り漁船が、呼子名物のいか活き造り用ケンサキイカを漁獲している。呼子朝市は漁港からすぐ近くの通りで毎日朝早くから開かれる。朝市の歴史は古く、大正時代初期に始まったとされる。

There is a good natural harbor in Yobuko, Karatsu City. It has prospered as a fishing village with favorable fishing position in the Genkainada nearby. Now,a lot of squid-fishing vessels provide swordtip squid for slices of a living squid, the specialty of Yobuko. Yobuko Morning Market is held on the street near the fishing port early in the morning every day. It has a long history from the early Taisho period.

所 〒847-0303　佐賀県唐津市呼子町呼子朝市通り
☎ 0955-82-0678　URL なし
Add: Asaichi-dori,Yobuko, Yobukocho, Karatsu, Saga 847-0303
Tel: 0955-82-0678　URL: Nothing

呼子はイカの町であり、またするめの町でもある。あたりを歩けばいか干し風景が見られる。ケンサキイカ(呼子ではヤリイカという)のするめは味のよさから「一番するめ」と呼ばれる。スルメイカ製のは「二番するめ」だ。

Yobuko is the town of squid, a lot of squid being dried around here and there. Dried swordtip squid is delicious, called "Ichiban-surume"(the top-grade dried squid). That of Japanese common flying squid is called "Niban-surume"(the second-grade one).

呼子朝市は千葉県勝浦と石川県輪島と並び、日本三大朝市の一つとされる。朝市通りの200メートルの商店前に堂々と露店が開かれる。漁師のおかみさんが魚介を並べ、農家の主婦が野菜や果物を売る。干物は自家製だ。

Yobuko Morning Market is one of the three major morning market in Japan which includes that of Katsu-ura and Wajima. The street stalls open confidently in front of shops on the Asaichi-Dori street which is 200 meters long.

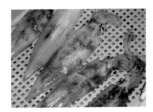

よく漁師のおかみさんがケンサキイカを売っている。獲ってきたばかりだからまだ生きていて、足がくにゃくにゃと動く。呼子の人はこれを買い求め、朝から呼子名物のいか活き造りに舌鼓を打つ。

The mistress of fishermen often sells swordtip squid. It is still alive with the legs moving because it has just been caught. Poking with a fingertip, beautiful spots spread out. A person who is good at cooking will buy it and people will smack their lips.

SWORDTIP SQUID

ケンサキイカ

KENSAKIIKA

剣先烏賊

いか活き造りにはケンサキイカが使われる。生け簀で泳いでいるのをすくいだしてすぐ造りにする。だからおいしい。

Swordtip squid is used for Ikizukuri, the slices of a live squid. It is made of a squid just caught in the fish live box.

NAHA

牧志公設市場/MAKISHI PUBLIC MARKET

沖縄県は亜熱帯性海域に浮かぶ160の島々からなる。沖合いには回遊魚の好漁場がある。島周辺の珊瑚礁海域では南方特有の魚介が漁獲される。牧志公設市場の鮮魚店には赤や青の原色に染まる魚がずらり。館内と周辺におよそ200の店がぎっしりと連なり、那覇市を代表する観光スポットになっている。

Okinawa Prefecture consists of 160 islands located in subtropical waters. There is a favorable fishery of migrating fish off the coast. The fishes specific to the south are caught in the sea area of coral reef. Fish dealers of the Makishi Public Market sell a lot of colorful fishes dyed primary colors like red and blue. About 200 shops line up densely in the building and around here, and this area is the representative sightseeing spots of Naha City.

所 〒900-0014　沖縄県那覇市松尾2-10-1
☎ 098-867-6560　URL https://kosetsu-ichiba.com/
Add: 2-10-1 Matsuo, Naha, Okinawa 900-0014
Tel: 098-867-6560　URL: https://kosetsu-ichiba.com/

1階には鮮魚店や食肉店、食料品店が密集し、アジアの熱気に満ちあふれる。鮮魚店で魚を買い求めて2階の食事処に持ち込み、調理代を払えば料理してくれる。持ち込みなしでも沖縄ならではの魚介料理や郷土料理が揃っている。

The first floor is crowded densely with fish dealers, meat shops and groceries and filled with enthusiasm of Asia. If you buy some fish there and bring it to the restaurant on the second floor, it can be cooked by the chef with a few extra charges. The restaurant serves Okinawa's unique seafoods dishes and local dishes, so you don not have bring any fishes.

南の海に多いカノコイセエビやニシキエビなどが「イセエビ」として並ぶ。カノコイセエビは形や大きさなどイセエビとよく似るが、色がやや紫がかっている。沖縄では刺身や鬼殻焼きなどイセエビ同様に食べられている。

Lobsters predominantly of the southern sea, such as Kanokoiseebi and Nishiki ebi, are sold as "Japanese spiny lobster". Kanokoiseebi is a little purplish to japanese spiny lobster. It is often eaten as sashimi and boiled one with shell.

STEEPHEAD PARROTFISH
ナンヨウブダイ

NANYOUBUDAI

南洋武鯛

ブダイの仲間。沖縄では「ゲンナーエラブチャー」、あるいは「オーバチャー」と呼ばれる。オスの額部が老魚になるほど前に突き出てくるから「かなづちぶだい」の名もある。「刺身」と呼ぶ酢味噌和えでよく食べられる。

It is called "Gennarerabuchar" or "Ohbachar" in Okinawa. Since the forehead of the male swells as growing up looks like a hammer, it is also called "Kanazuchi Budai (hammer parrotfish)". It is often, dressed with vinegar and miso, specially called "Sashimi".

What is brand-name fish?

ブランド魚とは？

日本にはブランド魚という特別の魚がある。多くが戦略によりブランドを定着させた魚のことだ。佐賀関（大分県）の「関さば」と「関あじ」が広く知られる。大分県漁協佐賀関支店の組合員が一本釣りで釣り上げたもの、消費地までは活き締めで運ばれたもの、などの条件を徹底することでその名を高めた。ほかに石巻（宮城県）の「金華かつお」「金華さば」などがある。それとは違って、古くからブランド力を持った魚もある。「城下がれい」（大分県）や「氷見ブリ」（富山県）などがそれだ。消費者にとってのブランド魚は安心でおいしい魚として期待できる。

There are some special fishes called "bland-name fish" in Japan. Most of them established the brand succeeding with branding strategy. Among them, "Sekisaba" and "Sekiaji" in Saganoseki (Oita Pref.) are well known. Its severe criteria for designation raises these reputation—to be caught by a member of Saganoseki Branch of Oita Fishermen's Cooperative with a fishing rod, to be delivered to the consumption area after immediately killed and so on. "Kinkakatsuo" and "Kinnkasaba" in Ishinomaki (Miyagi Pref.) are also this kind of brand-name fish. On the other hand, some fish has had brand power since long ago, such as "Jokagarei" (Oita Pref.) and "Himiburi" (Toyama Pref.). The brand name of fish ensures its safety and good taste to consumers.

Chapter

4

JAPANESE FISH DISHES

日本の魚料理

《魚料理を味わえる店》魚鐵 UOTETSU
〒102-0073 東京都千代田区九段北1-9-7　電話03-3261-3438
営業時間／11:30～14:00(L.O.13:30)、17:30～22:00(L.O.21:30)
定休日／土、日、祝　Add:1-9-7 Kudankita, Chiyoda-ku,
Tokyo,102-0073　Tel:03-3261-3438　Hours:11:30-14:00(L.
O.13:30), 17:30-22:00(L.O.21:30)　Closed:Saturdays,Sundays,
Holydays　※P102～106の料理

※この章は編集部が執筆

NIGIRI ZUSHI

握り寿司

寿司は、主に正月や祭り、婚礼など特別な
日に食べられた料理で、元は魚の保存食だ
った。塩づけにした魚介類を、ご飯と一緒
こつけて発酵させた「なれずし」が原型と
いわれ、米は食べずに捨てていた。江戸時
代後期になると、鮮魚の刺身と酢を混ぜた
ご飯を一緒に食べるようになり、これが握

Sushi is mainly had on special occasions such as new year's
festivals and weddings. It was originally a preservative seafood
dish. "Nare-zushi" which salt-pickled fish and seafood are fermented with rice is said its origin. Rice of Nare-sushi is discard-
ed. In the late Edo period, people start to eat fresh fish sashimi
with vinegared rice. It is considered as the beginning of Nigiri
zushi. Today, various kinds of seafoods from all over the world
are used for sushi and domestic regional fishes.

SASHIMI

刺身

鮮度の高い魚や貝の身を生のまま包丁でさばき、醤油やわさびにつけて味わう刺身。身の繊維に対して直角に切る「平造り」や、包丁を立てるようにして刃先で引くように薄く切る「細造り」など、包丁の切り方によって味も変わる。醤油で食べるほかに、漬け（づけ）にしたり、ショウガやニンニクといった薬味と一緒に食べたり、塩をふって酢でしめる調理法もある。刺身に添えられる大根などの「ツマ」は、抗菌効果や消化を助ける働きがある。

Sashimi is a dish to have fresh, raw fishes and clams cut with a knife and dipped into soy sauce and wasabi. By the cutting method of a knife such as "Hira-zukuri" which cuts the fish fiber at a right angle and "Hoso-zukuri" which slices the fish thin with the tip of the knife, the taste of sashimi differs. Other than soy sauce, sashimi is often eaten marinated, with seasoning like gingers and garlics or salt and vinegar pickled. Sashimi "garnish" which is made of Daikon radish is antibacterial and stimulates digestion.

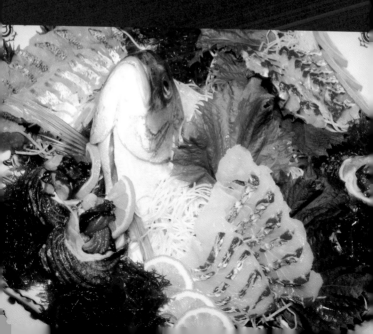

GRILLED FISH

焼き魚

火で炙るシンプルな魚料理。アジやサバといった大衆魚を焼き、塩で味付けする塩焼きのほかに、魚を原型のまま串刺しにして焼く姿焼きや醤油とみりんで味付けした照り焼きなどもある。焼き方は、「表六分に裏四分」。皮はパリッと、中身は水分が保たれたふっくらした身を味わえる。また「鯛の塩焼き」は、祝い事や節目の時にも登場し、正月の定番メニューとして食べられてきた。

A simple dish to grill a fish. Other than Shio-yaki to grill commonly eaten fishes such as horse mackerels and mackerels with salt, there are Sugata-yaki to skewer and grill an uncut fish, Teri-yaki to flavor fish with soy sauce and Mirin (sweet sake). To grill the top of the fish for 60% and back for 40% is the best to grill the skin crispy and the inside soft keeping the moist. Moreover, "Tai no Shio-yaki (a sea bream grilled with salt)" is served for festive occasions, life-stage events and popular dish of new year's.

SIMMERED FISH

煮魚

湯通しした魚を、醤油、酒、みりんなどで
煮た料理。調味料と煮ることで、味つけが
され、身が柔らかくなる。魚によって煮方
が異なり、白身魚は薄味であっさりと仕上
げ、青魚やマグロなど脂の多い魚はやや濃
いめで甘辛く味付けする。サバなど、魚に
よっては味噌と一緒に煮たり、野菜を加え
て煮たりする。昔から日常食として家庭で
食べられてきたが、近年の研究では、古代
では儀礼の時のごちそうとして使われてき
たという。

A dish to simmer a blanched fish with soy sauce, sake and mirin.
By simmering with the seasoning, the fish is flavored and soft-
ened. Simmering method differs by fishes. White-fleshed fishes
should be flavored lightly. Fatty fishes like blue-fleshed fishes
and tuna should be flavored a bit strong salty sweet taste. Some
fishes like mackerels are simmered with miso and adding vegetables. It has been a popular home-style dish for a long time, how-
ever, by the recent research, it was known the dish was served
as a ceremonial dish in an ancient time.

STEAMED IN SAKE

酒蒸し

名に"蒸し"とあるが、強火で貝のふたが開くまで"蒸し煮"にする料理。酒で蒸し煮にするため貝の臭みが消え、旨味が引き出される。火にかけることでアルコールが飛び、煮汁は飲むこともできるため、最後の一滴まで貝の旨味を堪能できる。お酒との相性がよく、つきみとして好まれる。アサリの

It is said "mushi (steamed)", but it is a dish to Braise clams with high heat until they open. Since clams are Braised with sake, odor is rid, and flavor is stood out. By cooking with heat, alcohol is cooked out, so you can drink the soup and enjoy the flavor of the clams to the last drop. The dish matches with alcohol drinks, so it is popular as nibbles. Other than Asari clams, common orient clams and oysters are also used. On the other hand, there are steamed dishes to cook with steam using steamers.

TEMPURA
天ぷら

エビやイカ、白身魚などのタネに衣をつけ、油で揚げる料理。衣に包むことで、タネの旨味を閉じ込めることができる。揚げる時は火加減を一定に保つと、ふわっとした食感を保ちながら、タネに十分に火が通るので、独特の食感も楽しめる。関東と関西で違いがあり、関東では主に魚に卵を入れた衣をつけて揚げ、関西では野菜に小麦粉だけの衣をつけて揚げるのが特徴。約480年前にポルトガルから伝わった料理とされる。

A dish to deep-fry shrimps, squids, and white-fleshed fishes in batter. By battering, the flavor of seafoods is sealed in. Maintaining the heat of cooking constant keeps the soft texture and cooks the seafoods thoroughly, so you can enjoy the unique texture of it. It differs between Kanto and Kansai. In Kanto region, tempura is mainly fishes with eggs in batter and cooked. In Kansai region, only flour is used in batter and cooked. It is said tempura is brought from Portugal about 480 years ago.

ARAJIRU
あら汁

魚をさばいた時に残った頭や中骨などを
"あら"と呼び、それを使った汁物。鯛やブ
リなど、大振りな魚でつくることが多い。
魚のあらに湯をかけて臭みをとり、ショウ
ガ汁とともに煮出し、最後に三つ葉で彩り
を加える。味付けは塩だけで、魚本来の旨
味を堪能できる。見た目も作り方もシンプ
ルだが、魚の素材の味を余すところなく味
わえる。ほかにも、味噌や醤油、粕仕立て
で味付けし、根菜やこんにゃく、練り物な

A soup cooked with remaining parts after cutting a fish like its
head and bones called "Ara". Large fishes such as sea breams
and yellowtails are often used. Blanching Ara to rid the odor and
boiling it with Ginger soup, and then adding a color with Japanese honeworts. Only with salt, you can enjoy the flavor of fish itself. It is a simple dish with the look and recipe, but you can taste
the fish thoroughly. Additionally, miso, soy sauce or sake lees are
used as flavoring. Moreover, root vegetables, konnyaku (yam
cakes) and fish-paste loaves are also added.

HOT POT

鍋料理

複数人でひとつの鍋を囲んで食べる、冬の定番料理。サケ、アンコウ、ブリ、フグといった白身魚やエビ、貝類を水や昆布の出汁とともに煮る。調味料は醤油か味噌が一般的。アサリやシジミなどの貝類なら、出汁さえ使わないこともある。煮ることで具材の旨味が汁に煮出されるので、〆に麺やご飯を汁に入れて食べる。組み合わせは自由で、北海道の石狩鍋、福井のカニちり、山口のフグちりなど、食材の相性を考えた鍋料理が全国で楽しめる。

A popular winter dish to share one pot of cooking. To boil white-fleshed fishes like salmons, monkfishes, yellowtails and blow-fishes, shrimps or clams in water and seaweed soup stock. Generally, soy sauce or miso is used as the seasoning. If clams such as Asari and Shijimi is used, soup stock might not be necessary. By boiling it, flavor of the ingredients is extracted in the soup, so noodles or rice are added and served as a closing dish of the meal. There is no rule for the choice of ingredients. You can enjoy well-balanced nabe dishes all over Japan such as Ishikari-nabe in Hokkaido, Kani-chiri in Fukui and Fugu-chiri in Yamaguchi.

SAKANA WORDS
用語集

Katugyo
活魚

調理されるまで生きた状態で運ばれる魚介類。

Live fish. It is delivered alive until cooked.

Sengyo
鮮魚

とれたての新鮮な魚。活魚と違い、魚は死んでいる。

Fresh fish which is freshly caught. Unlike live fish, it is dead.

Mekiki
目利き

魚介類の種類や品質を見分けること。それに優れた人。

The judgement of kinds and qualities of seafood. / A person who is a good judge.

Aitaiuri
相対売り

売り手と買い手が話し合って値段を決めて売買する方法。

A cross trade that a seller and a buyer negotiate the price.

Asa (morning)
朝

市場では夜が明けないうちから「朝」という。21時頃を「早朝」という人もいる。

In the market, people call a period of time before the night ends, "morning". Some people call about 9 o'clock at night, "early morning".

Turret Truck

ターレ（ターレットトラック）

市場で見かける、円筒形の動力部が回転する独特な形をした運搬車。

A carrying vehicle in the market. It has a unique shape that the cylindrical power device rotates.

Seri

せり

購入希望者が値段を競い、もっとも高い値段を示した人が買うのが「上げぜり」。設定金額から値段を下げていき、買い手がついたところで取引が成立する「下げぜり」。希望者が一度だけ金額を提示し、もっとも高い値段を示した人が買える「一発ぜり」などがある。

Seri means an auction. The auction that purchase candidates compete on price and the highest bidder buys it is "Agezeri". The one that an auctioneer lowers the price and the deal is concluded when finding a buyer is "Sagezeri".

Tane / Neta

タネ・ネタ

寿司や天ぷらの材料になる魚介類などのこと。「タネ」が正しい言葉で、「ネタ」は隠語。

Seafood which is used for sushi and templa. The correct way to say it is "Tane" and "Neta" is a cant.

Syusseuo

出世魚

成長にしたがって名前が変わる魚。縁起の良い魚として祝宴の料理に好んで使われる。

Fish that are called by different names as they grow larger. It is a popular feast menu as it is thought to be a good omen.

CONCLUSION

おわりに

　私は全国の浜をほっつき歩いては漁師料理や漁業、魚を取材して雑誌に寄稿し、また本にまとめてきました。そんな取材をかれこれ40年以上！　それでも漁師さんやおかみさんたちが語る蘊蓄話や自慢話に飽きることがありません。なかでも浜の料理は奥が深く、ますます興味を募らせています。今日では江戸前寿司や日本食が世界的に評判を高めています。しかし日本の魚料理はそれだけではありません。長く受け継がれてきた郷土料理や家庭料理にも、魚の魅力ある食べ方が数多くあります。本書を読み終えたみなさまが、日本のおいしい魚に出会うことを切に願っています。

野村祐三

I have wandered about coasts all over Japan, collected information about fishermen's dishes, fishery and fishes and then written for magazines and books. It's been more than 40 years! Still, I never get bored with listening to the extensive knowledge and boasts of fishermen's and their wives. Among them, the beachside recipe is really profound and increasingly attracts me. Nowadays, Edomae-sushi and Japanese cuisine raise the worldwide reputation, but they are not the only things of Japanese dish of fish. There are a lot of ways of enjoy eating fishes in local and homemade cuisine, which have long been passed down. I earnestly hope that you will meet delicious Japanese fishes after reading this book.

Yuzo Nomura

野村 祐三（のむら・ゆうぞう）

昭和20年、中国太原市生まれ。フリーランスライターとして全国の漁師を取材し、地魚料理、漁業、食全般の記事を各誌に寄稿。主な著書は『ブランド魚入門』（祥伝社）、『東北さかな紀行』（無明舎出版）、『旬のうまい魚を知る本』（東京書籍）、『豪快にっぽん漁師料理』（集英社）、『英語と日本語で紹介する 寿司ネタの魚がわかる本』（講談社）。

※ Chapter4 のみ編集部が執筆を担当。

Designer・DTP	佐々木志帆（ナイスク naisg.com）
Editor	松尾里央、岸正章、河野将、柴田由美（ナイスク naisg.com）
Edit Cooperation	川口明日香
Illustrator	山口正児
Translator	石田康衣、亀濱香
Photographer	小原孝博、山根衣理
Special Thanks	魚鐵、越後村上うおや、沖縄県漁業協同組合連合会、カクダイ水産株式会社、水産研究・教育機構 および 水産庁、東京都中央卸売市場、焼津さかなセンター

the SAKANA&TSUKIJI BOOK
魚&築地市場ガイドブック《英語対訳つき》

2018年6月25日 初版 第1刷発行

著者	野村祐三
発行者	岩野裕一
発行所	株式会社実業之日本社
	〒153-0044 東京都目黒区大橋1-5-1 クロスエアタワー8階
	［編集］電話 03-6809-0452
	［販売］電話 03-6809-0495
	［URL］http://www.j-n.co.jp/

印刷・製本 大日本印刷株式会社